PRAISE FOR *TINY BUDDHA'S GUIDE TO LOVING YOURSELF*

"Loving yourself is the foundation for finding inner peace, happiness, and the ability to love others. In this wonderful book, Lori Deschene does something remarkable. She makes the topic of loving yourself come alive in a way that is both highly entertaining and very practical. This is one book that shouldn't be missed."

—JONATHAN ROBINSON, founder of
FindingHappiness.com and the author of *Communication Miracles for Couples*

"You have to love yourself to love other people and your life. In this powerful collection of stories and insights, Lori Deschene and other Tiny Buddha contributors share how they overcome shame, insecurity, and perfectionism to help you do just that. I highly recommend *Tiny Buddha's Guide to Loving Yourself* to anyone who needs a little help recognizing their worth and potential."

—KAREN SALMANSOHN, bestselling author of *Prince Harming Syndrome*

"This wonderful collection of personal stories and words of wisdom will help you become kinder and more compassionate to yourself, and ultimately show you how to lead a happier and more fulfilling life."

—KRISTIN NEFF, author of *Self-Compassion, Stop Beating Yourself Up* and *Leave Insecurity Behind*

"We can all feel broken, wounded, and alone at times, but never while reading this beautiful, wise guide to taking good care of ourselves. Some of us need permission to do that. All of us can find inspiration and powerful lessons in *Tiny Buddha's* openhearted, generous community of teachers. I'm so grateful to have found them."

—PRISCILLA WARNER, author of *Learning to Breathe: My Yearlong Quest to Bring Calm to My Life*

"Reading Lori Deschene's wonderful new book, *Tiny Buddha's Guide to Loving Yourself*, is like listening to a good friend who reminds you of who you are when you need to hear it the most. Deschene and her contributors write about real-life situations with real-life solutions and they do it with the same unflinching honesty that has made TinyBuddha.com so popular. If you are ever hard on yourself—and who isn't—you need to read this book."

—AMANDA OWEN, author of *The Power of Receiving*

PRAISE FOR *TINY BUDDHA, SIMPLE WISDOM FOR LIFE'S HARD QUESTIONS*

"How can we find happiness and peace—right now, right here? In her engaging, thought-provoking book *Tiny Buddha*, Lori Deschene explores this enormous question to help readers grapple with challenges like money, love, pain, control, and meaning, in order to find greater happiness."

—GRETCHEN RUBIN, author of *The Happiness Project*

"Lori is one of a kind. Her amazing heart and wisdom shine through in everything she writes! I am a HUGE fan of *Tiny Buddha*, and I'm constantly inspired by Lori and her work."

—MASTIN KIPP, founder of The Daily Love
(thedailylove.com)

"There's nothing tiny about the extra-large dose of awesome stuffed into Lori's writing. Read it and feel good about the world."

—NEIL PASRICHA, founder and author of *1000 Awesome Things* and *The Book of Awesome*

"Few people in our time have more passionately or more creatively applied wisdom teachings to a new digital generation than Lori Deschene. I am continually inspired by her writing, and also by her sincere dedication to learning, growth, and wisdom. I feel tremendously fortunate to have had the chance to get to know her work through *Tiny Buddha*, and to know her as a person. Both embody the same essential truths."

—SOREN GORDHAMER, founder and author of *Wisdom 2.0*

"Lori Deschene doesn't claim to be anybody's guru. But it's that lack of pretense and her total candor—how she tells her own often-wild story without flinching—that is so magnetic, inviting a sense of ease with our own wrinkles, too, and fostering a sense of personal possibility. As she asks: Are you ready to be free?"

—MARGARET ROACH, author of *And I Shall Have Some Peace There*

"*Tiny Buddha* is a moving and insightful synthesis of evocative stories and ancient wisdom applied to modern life. A great read!"

—JONATHAN FIELDS, author of *Uncertainty*

"I spent months retweeting posts from a mystery handle called @tinybuddha. I wasn't the only one: Hundreds of thousands of people followed the daily messages. I was intrigued and made it a point to meet the woman behind the message. Today, Lori Deschene is a friend and fellow author who spreads truth and inspiration throughout the twittersphere, her blog, and now her new book! Lori has shifted the energy of the Internet with her loving daily posts and now she is sharing more with the world throughout her incredible book!"

—GABRIELLE BERNSTEIN, author of
Add More –ing to your Life and *Spirit Junkie*

TINY BUDDHA'S GUIDE TO LOVING YOURSELF

40 Ways
to Transform Your Inner Critic *and* Your Life

LORI DESCHENE

Conari Press

Cover Design: Elina Diaz
Layout & Design: Maureen Forys, Happenstance Type-O-Rama

For permission requests, please contact the publisher at:
Mango Publishing Group
2850 S Douglas Road, 2nd Floor
Coral Gables, FL 33134 USA
info@mango.bz

For special orders, quantity sales, course adoptions and corporate sales, please email the publisher at sales@mango.bz. For trade and wholesale sales, please contact Ingram Publisher Services at customer.service@ingramcontent.com or +1.800.509.4887.

Tiny Buddha's Guide to Loving Yourself : 40 Ways to Transform Your Inner Critic and Your Life

Library of Congress Cataloging-in-Publication data
ISBN: (p) 978-1-64250-302-9 (e) 978-1-64250-303-6
BISAC category code PHI028000, PHILOSOPHY / Buddhist

Printed in the United States of America

In loving memory of Jeanne "Grambo" Santoro.
You weren't just loveable; you were love, in its purest, rarest form.

CONTENTS

ACKNOWLEDGMENTS

For every book, there are innumerable people to thank, but in this one there are forty times as many. First and foremost, thank you to all of the contributors who shared their stories and insights. I'm inspired by your honesty and vulnerability, and grateful to have learned from you. Thank you also to all of the family members, friends, and teachers who have touched your lives and helped shape you into the beautiful people you are.

To my family, including but not limited to Kevin, Marianne, Tara, Ryan, Pauline, Cassie, Pat, Jim, and Justin, who will live on in all of our hearts (and my many aunts, uncles, and cousins, both Deschene- and Santoro-descended), thank you for being kind, supportive, generous, funny, and always entertaining. I'm grateful that from the east to the west, I'm surrounded by laughter and love. To Jan, Pat, Susie, Vanessa, and the rest of the team at Conari, thank you for all your efforts in making another Tiny Buddha book come to life. To Joshua Denney of Think Web Strategy, thank you for not only being a gifted designer, but also for being available for around-the-clock Skype chats, whether related to Tiny Buddha or not.

And last but certainly not least, thank you to Ehren for letting me read and re-read the same thing twenty times even after I only changed a few words; for always being willing to give me advice, knowing I sometimes may seek but not follow it; and for being such a huge part of Tiny Buddha's heart—and an even bigger part of mine.

ABOUT TINY BUDDHA AND THIS BOOK

WE ARE NOT ALONE WITH WHAT WE'RE GOING THROUGH. THAT'S the core message behind tinybuddha.com, a community blog that features stories and lessons from people of all ages from all over the world. It's a place where we can come together to share our struggles and successes, knowing that despite our unique life circumstances, we're really not all that different. No matter what we do, what we believe, where we've been, or where we're going, we all want to be happy, we all want to move beyond our pain, and we all have infinite potential, if only we're willing to believe it.

In the past three years, more than five hundred and fifty people have contributed stories to the site, many exploring their experiences in forgiving, accepting, and even celebrating who they are right now. What always strikes me about the posts people share is how brave they are in acknowledging the feelings and experiences many of us might be tempted to hide. Once one person has put it out there it's so much easier to admit that we've been there too. It's a tremendous relief to realize that whatever we're feeling, it's okay. We're okay. We don't have to fight it. We just have to acknowledge it, try to understand it instead of judging it, and then use that understanding to grow through and beyond it.

I decided to create this book as a collaborative effort, including forty blog posts from tinybuddha.com, for that reason. So much of our resistance to loving ourselves has to do with shame—the thought that there's something wrong with us for what we're going through. These posts have reminded me, and more than a million monthly readers, that we are never alone, and we *can* change our thoughts and our lives. They touch upon ideas that will help you:

- Release shame about your past and the limiting beliefs that keep you stuck

- See yourself as beautiful and valuable, with all your flaws and weaknesses

- Accept yourself more and judge yourself less

- Forgive yourself for your mistakes and stop being hard on yourself

- Minimize the need for approval to feel more confident

- Let go of the comparisons that keep you feeling inferior

- Feel complete so that you no longer look to others to fill a void within yourself

- Find the courage to share your authentic self for deeper connections with others

- Learn to take care of yourself instead of putting everyone else's needs first

- Believe that you're valuable so you can start creating a life you love

I've categorized the posts into ten chapters, connected to each of these themes, and then written an introduction for each one. Though I ordered the stories in a way that made sense to me, you don't need to read each chapter sequentially if you'd rather skip to sections that feel most relevant for you. I tried to choose a balanced selection of posts that pertain to our environment, relationships, and even work—all the different facets of our lives that stand to improve when we begin to love ourselves in action.

You'll notice that, unlike in my first book, I don't share any of my own stories in the chapter introductions. Beyond what I share in the early pages regarding who I am and how this book came to be, I wanted to keep the focus on the contributors' stories and lessons.

Some of the posts share vulnerable stories; others are more instructive than personally revealing; but all contain such strong insights that I felt compelled to include them. Many of the stories come from people who have experienced some type of mistreatment that they then learned to emulate through patterns of addiction. Others come from people who came from healthier backgrounds but still adopted self-diminishing habits that they've recognized and confronted. Even if you don't relate to all the stories, some will sound familiar to you, and I hope there will be lessons from each one that you can apply to your own experience.

At the end of each chapter you'll find four tips—one from each of the four posts in that section. I advise you to look at the forty tips not as things you need to do as you read, but as ideas you can turn to whenever you need help changing your thoughts, and consequently, your feelings and experience of the world. That's the point of this book. It's not about forty simple action steps to change you life; it's about forty simple ways you can change your mindset right now. That, I've learned, is what changes our lives: doing our best *right now,* and as best we can in the nows to come.

ABOUT MY JOURNEY TO THIS BOOK

I'VE OFTEN SAID THAT I PRACTICALLY POPPED OUT OF THE WOMB crying, "Look at me!" followed immediately by, "What are you looking at?" For most of my life, I felt a desperate need to receive pure attention underscored by insecurity about what people would see. It was the deep, all-consuming need for validation punctuated by the fear that I wasn't worthy of it. I felt lacking, less than, lost, lonely, and completely powerless to change.

On the long, winding road to a mind less cruel, I've learned that a lot of us desperately want to know what love and happiness feel like, but we don't really believe we deserve either. And we also have no idea how to give them to ourselves. We're so used to beating ourselves up over mistakes, blaming ourselves for everything we've failed to do, and doubting what we can do in the future that we believe we need our punishing inner voice. If only it pushes us hard enough, maybe we'll become better. And then maybe we'll feel better. Maybe we'll find a place somewhere on the other side of self-judgment where we can finally accept ourselves and enjoy our lives.

But it doesn't actually work that way. We can't hate ourselves into a version of ourselves we can love. Before we can feel good about who we are, we have to choose to be good to ourselves, just as we are. You may have learned to do the exact opposite in your childhood or beyond. And as a result, you may have spent the majority of your life trying to fix yourself, win approval from everyone around you, and escape the shame of your worst decisions. I collected these stories and wrote this book because I know the pain of that reality all too well—and I know there is another way.

In hindsight, I see that I lived most of my early life mired in a deep sense of self-loathing. I thought I felt so empty and lonely because the world was against me. I had lots of evidence to prove the world is a harsh, uncaring place—that people would hurt me if I let my guard down. But I hurt myself more by keeping it up, because the space in which I isolated myself was far more cruel and toxic. No other person could be as mean to me as I was; no one else's opinion of me could be more judgmental than my own; and nothing in the unknown could be more painful than the familiarity of my self-induced suffering.

I was twenty-one when a therapist asked me to draw a self-portrait. I'd spent the ten years prior writing my feelings in journals, though I rarely felt anything for long. I had a vast collection of worn, faded diaries, all venting my anger at the ways others had hurt me and chronicling the many ways I'd hurt myself in response. What started as an adolescent escape from cruelty turned into a log for everything related to self-torture.

Five hundred. That's the number of calories I felt comfortable digesting each day in an attempt to control my body—one of the only things I felt I could control. Thirteen. That's the highest number of times I threw up on a given day to rid myself of anything in excess of that. Thirty. That's the minimum number of times I weighed myself each day to ensure my weight hadn't exceeded ninety-nine pounds. Ten. That's the approximate number of times I passed out on my college campus, causing my peers and teachers to worry for my well-being. Six. That's how many times I ended up in the ER, dehydrated, with chest pains that I feared might be a heart attack. Seven. That's how many inpatient hospitals kicked me out, with doctors convinced I was beyond help. Three. That's how many months I spent at a residential treatment center in Wisconsin, where I sat in art therapy, pencil in hand, tasked with drawing myself as I saw me.

I started by drawing a circle that was puckered at the top, as if cinched. Inside I drew gray matter—something colorless and almost fluid. It was a crude drawing without much detail; other people likely wouldn't know what it was. That seemed to be an accurate representation of myself; I didn't know what I was made of, either. But everyone in that room knew I saw myself as the contents of that bag. It was a visual depiction of my most shameful memory to date.

At twelve years old, I'd felt ugly and inferior. It wasn't just that I was chubbier, less popular, and less talented than my older sister, who attracted boys like I never did. It wasn't the scoliosis back brace that consistently failed to make me straight. It wasn't that many of my peers seemed to confirm my lack of intrinsic value. It was my belief that I was unworthy of love. Still, I always fought to get it, and I thought one surefire way was to pretend I had an eating disorder.

I'd seen an after school special about two girls—one anorexic and one bulimic—and it seemed that everyone in their lives paid attention to them. I didn't focus on the fact that the bulimic died in the end, though that was a fate that didn't scare me, since I was convinced my life was worthless. I just wanted people to notice me. I wanted to do something so dangerous and terrifying that people had to stop and focus solely on me. It was a selfish, ignorant desire, but I remember the first time I threw up thinking that I was only acting. I wasn't *actually* bulimic. I was just doing a really good job of playing this role for attention.

I wanted to look like someone who was helpless, and eventually, I was. By college, my whole life revolved around my secret bulimic ritual. It would start with feeling—anything. Guilt. Anger. Regret. Mostly shame. But sometimes even happiness, since I felt I didn't deserve it, or feared I couldn't hold on to it. From there came the eating—mindless self-stuffing, devoid of pleasure or satisfaction. It was carnal, frenzied, violent even, an attempt to anesthetize myself. And for a moment, nothing hurt. There were no thoughts, just the hunt for food and the mission to consume it as quickly as possible without anyone else finding out. I was there, but not—in my body, but out of my head. It was half of a process that had to be completed, and that caused me a great deal of anxiety, the fear I may not be able to empty the hole I'd temporarily filled.

After years of hiding my binging and purging cycle, and years of others trying to interrupt it, I knew there was always the possibility I wouldn't be able to finish. I knew I might not be able to regain control and feel the release that was my drug. The popped blood vessels in my eyes, the bloody scrapes on my knuckles, the decay in my teeth—these signs betrayed that I was still doing it, but I'd gotten creative at hiding it, as I did in my final inpatient hospitalization.

Since I'd already been thrown out of the only eating disorder ward in Massachusetts, I found myself in several psychiatric units, each incapable of effectively treating me. No one on staff possessed the knowledge or ability to provide me with the help I needed—but really, I wasn't open to receiving it, not from my family and not from them. In that last hospital, they left me unsupervised at meals and then locked me in my room. I'd have free reign over a fully stocked kitchen for breakfast, lunch, and dinner before a staffer escorted me to torturous solitude where I inevitably felt unhinged.

There came a time when I couldn't breathe. I'd spent thirty minutes sitting barefoot in a sweat suit, with other patients in the kitchen. Since my neighbor had tried to hang herself with a shoelace, none of us were allowed to keep ours. I could hear her screaming from down the hall, but it was nothing compared to the noise in my head. I couldn't believe this was where my life had gone. I couldn't believe I was here and not well on my way to graduating from college. Mostly, I couldn't believe that I'd soon be locked in a room where I wouldn't be able to rid myself of the toxicity inside me.

I panicked. I decided I had to do it. Every second that went by was one second closer to digestion—one heartbeat closer to losing control. I had to be empty again. If I allowed myself to feel that sense of powerlessness, all the pain from all the other times I'd felt the same would wash over me like a tidal wave. That bag I drew in art therapy—it was the hollowed out pillow inside a case that I'd convinced a young girl to smuggle out of my room after I'd purged into it.

I'd knocked on the locked door, telling a nearby mental health counselor that I needed my friend to get my laundry. I knew the pillow hadn't made it to the trash when I sat before one of the counselors in his office. He told me I should be ashamed of myself, and that it was time for me to leave. With those words echoing in my head, I considered that perhaps I should just give up. I *deserved* to feel ashamed. I did horrible, reprehensible things. I was selfish and weak. These were the beliefs I'd spent the decade prior trying to numb—that the times when others bullied, intimidated, and berated me, I'd brought it on myself. And yet, somewhere inside me, I held on to hope that I was so much more than the worst things I had done; that's the part of me that located the residential treatment center and begged them to accept me.

I left Wisconsin after three months of intensive treatment not completely healed, but with my most life-threatening behaviors either eliminated or dramatically reduced. I had started ascending from the depths of my self-loathing, but the reality was I had a long way to go. No longer was I slowly dying, but I had no idea what it meant to really live. I only knew I wanted to get far away from everything that reminded me of who I'd been. So I left—moved as far away as I could without leaving the country, from the East to the West Coast. After a decade of therapy and medications, I now lived in a world without either. That was the beginning of a new kind of healing, and it brought me all around the United States as I moved and traveled for work, trying to discover who I could be.

Looking back, I see it hasn't been a linear journey, every day better than the one prior. It's been a process of two steps forward, one step back. I've gone through many periods of confusion, desperation, and self-doubt. I've also impressed myself, inspired myself, and enjoyed myself like I was rarely able to do when my life revolved around being sick.

There came a time, six years back, when I returned to Wisconsin to share my story with new residents. As I stood in front of the room—eyes clear, hand unmarked, skin pink instead of sallow—I shared some of the many self-destructive things I'd once done in secrecy. Then I recounted the words a mental health counselor once told me, after I'd sunk to a new low: You should be ashamed of yourself.

I told them he was wrong. Yes, I'd made a big mistake. Yes, I'd done selfish, dangerous things. Yes, I needed to take responsibility for my life instead of drowning in my victim mentality. But if I hoped to do that, I had to challenge the voice inside that told me I should feel ashamed. I had to see myself more as the light I'd shuttered for years and less as the darkness that threatened to suffocate it. I had to start telling the story of my strength instead of dwelling on the stories of my former weakness. That, right there, is why I never again told this story, until now: I no longer wanted to build my identity around my eating disorder. I didn't want it to be how you defined me. But I now realize it doesn't matter if you choose to define me by the lowest lows of my past; what matters is how I define myself through my actions in the present.

This, I've learned, is the foundation of self-love: knowing that we are so much more than our greatest mistakes, our weakest moments, or our most shameful decisions; and realizing that we can be who we want to be right now, not just in spite of where we've been, but also because of it.

I share these specifics from my own journey now knowing full well that you, the reader, may never have hated yourself quite so intensely. You may never have come close to death, or wished for your death, or wondered if the people in your life would be better off without you. But this is part of my truth. Though it took me a long time to realize it, these feelings of unworthiness caused all the pain in my life—not the relationships that didn't work out or the many jobs that didn't feel fulfilling. Nothing ever felt good enough because I didn't believe *I* was good enough. That, I suspect, may resonate with you too.

It's something most of us have in common: We don't fully believe we are as beautiful and loveable as we are. Just as we may find proof that we can't trust other people, we search for evidence that supports our distorted perceptions of ourselves. And so it goes inside our heads, the cyclical negative thoughts about who we are, what we think we've done wrong, and what we wish we could change but fear we can't. Everything that happens externally reflects what goes on internally. The good news is that we all have the power to change one by starting to change the other.

It's this realization (among others) that prompted me to start tinybuddha.com in 2009 as a space where we can all learn to heal, and not just survive, but thrive. It's also what led me to this book. Every single one of us has amazing potential to create purpose, passion, and joy in life, but first we need to believe we deserve it.

You do.

Even if you've made choices you wouldn't make based on what you know now, you don't deserve to feel inadequate, ashamed, unworthy, or inferior to anyone else. You don't deserve the anguish of beating yourself up over the past, or the insatiable emptiness that comes from believing you're fundamentally lacking. No matter where you've been, you deserve the opportunity to go where you're going less burdened by your own mind.

This means not only being good to yourself, but also cutting yourself some slack when you struggle with that. I've learned that we may never completely eliminate self-doubting and self-critical thoughts, but it's possible to think them a lot less often, and to give them less power when we do. And there's great power in this gradual, imperfect journey. Tiny shifts in our minds can create massive change in our lives. I hope this book helps you be a little easier on you and a little more present and joyful in your life, one thought and one moment at a time.

CHAPTER 1

When You're Stuck in Your Childhood: Moving Beyond What You Learned

So much of how we feel about ourselves pertains to our experiences as children. If you didn't grow up with love and support, odds are you've struggled to offer those things to yourself and others around you. If the people who were supposed to care for you neglected your emotional or physical needs, you probably concluded that your needs weren't important—and that you somehow deserved to be ignored.

Ironically, if you grew up in an abusive environment, you may have felt overwhelming anger toward people who hurt you, only to grow up and adopt their voice in your head. That's the paradox of mistreatment: you may feel outraged when you recognize you've been wronged, and yet pick up where your abusers left off. We often treat ourselves the only way we know how—the way we learned through example from our parents and/or peers.

For those who didn't experience abuse growing up, you likely still formed conclusions about yourself based on your relationship with your parents. Many of us learned at a young age that love, acceptance, and approval were conditional on certain behaviors and achievements. But we didn't conclude that our *behaviors* weren't good enough; we internalized it to mean that *we* weren't—that there was something innately wrong with us. According to psychotherapist and researcher Alice J. Brown, author of *Core Beliefs Psychotherapy,* because we're egocentric as children, we assume that when our parents aren't there for us, we're somehow to blame.

As adults, we may understand that we did not deserve to feel bad and that we shouldn't torture ourselves for things other people have done. But sometimes despite knowing these things, we don't fully believe them. We don't grasp that we've always been beautiful, even if we've never been perfect, and that we've never deserved to feel scared, alone, or ashamed—not when we were kids, and not now.

It's helpful to understand how our childhood experiences shaped us, but it's not about placing blame or playing the victim. It's about recognizing that *we all* learned to question ourselves, on some level, growing up—even those of us who had the most attentive parents, since various factors contribute to our beliefs about ourselves. And we can all learn to love, support, and nurture ourselves now, regardless of how we've struggled. We can all challenge our thoughts and beliefs to cultivate positive feelings about ourselves—flaws and all.

How do we let go of the stories that we've been clinging to for years? How can we begin to move beyond trauma and pain? How can we release our shame and start recognizing our worth and beauty? Countless Tiny Buddha contributors have addressed these questions on the site, sharing their experiences and insights. Some of those include . . .

OPENING YOURSELF UP TO LOVE WHEN YOU DIDN'T GROW UP WITH IT

by Marie

> *You, yourself, as much as anybody in the entire universe, deserve your love and affection.*
>
> —BUDDHA

I've always craved love and attention. This is not to say that I accepted love willingly—quite the opposite, in fact. If someone decided to like or even love me they would have to pass through a path of obstacles, being pushed, pulled, and tested at every corner. Only then, upon arrival at the finish line, would they gain my acceptance.

As you can imagine, this eliminated a number of potential friends and partners, and I often found myself lonely and disappointed. The root of my inability to accept love easily stems from my childhood. My mother was unable to connect with me. She got pregnant during the height of her modeling career. After she gave birth, her career dried up. She resented the attention that a baby attracted, and, in addition to this, she was highly addicted to narcotics.

Growing up with my mother telling me that she felt no love and was ashamed of me made me desperate to be the perfect daughter. I would go to any length to prove myself worthy, even taking drugs with her as a way of connecting. When I was fifteen years old, she upped and left with no good-bye, leaving me with my stepdad and an overwhelming sense of failure. If my own mother could not love me, how and why would anyone else?

After my mother left, I disguised my pain through drugs and control. Drugs provided an instant, closely bonded social network. I tried to take control through self-harm. My life continued like this for ten years. I hated myself, and I was terrified of letting anyone in. Throughout these years, I did several stints in rehabilitation centers, where nurses and psychiatrists worked hard on me. I would almost give in and build connections with these people, but when the time came to leave these institutions I would find myself alone all over again.

I was desperate for a loving relationship and a career. My battles were hindering me from achieving either. Luckily, I had a fantastic education under my belt, through a childhood spent at top boarding schools. It was just a matter of escaping this vicious cycle that I had spent the majority of my life spinning around in. I had stopped the drugs, but I was addicted to self-pity. Therapy had taught me that I needed to let go and learn to trust. This sounds quite easy now, but back then the very idea was not only terrifying but also impossible.

I always dreaded birthdays and holidays. On my twenty-fifth birthday I woke up with an annual feeling of dread. I went to the store to buy some cigarettes, and the lady at the counter asked me for some identification. I handed it over and she said to me "It's your birthday today. You look so young. Your mother should be very proud of you."

It was such a simple compliment, but for some reason it struck a chord. After all my years of therapy, these words from a stranger hit home. I can't really explain it, but I felt a whole hoard of emotions release: anger, regret, understanding, and, finally, relief. I felt that, yes, my mother should be proud of me, and I felt sorry for her that she was unable to feel that way.

I wanted to have a chance at life, to meet someone and have my own children who I could love and be proud of. I realized then that this would only happen if I stopped treating myself the same way my mother did. Considering how long and hard it was to reach this point, turning my life around was surprisingly easy. The hardest point was the realization.

If your parents didn't treat you well, and you'd like to treat yourself better and open up to love, I recommend that you:

Write through your fears and feelings. I didn't want to cause myself any more harm; I wanted to connect and understand how I worked instead. Writing things down served as a great release.

Go out and get a journal with the main intention of putting your emotions into words. Try and pinpoint when and what makes you feel good or sad. By putting everything on paper, you can then reference your emotions, look into your behavioral patterns, and recognize what made you feel a certain way and how you dealt with it. Keeping a journal keeps you connected to yourself so you can make real changes that last.

Risk trusting other people. Instead of testing people in my life, I let go and granted people access. This was a difficult step, as rejection is way out of my comfort zone. However, I put myself on the line and trusted my instincts. I decided that even if someone let me down, I could handle it. Moving into different social circles helped. I got back in touch with people I liked growing up, and I was surprised to find that a number of them were happy to reconnect with me. As I started to feel more connected and less alone, I realized this paid off.

I also decided to be open with new people who came into my life. I didn't scare them off at the first encounter, but as relationships began to develop, I would explain how my past affected me, and how I'd chosen to move on and be happy. Almost everyone I opened up to was completely supportive. Openness became a two-way street. I learned that most people have experienced their own struggles. Our confessions strengthened these new relationships. I also learned that not everyone is someone I can open up to—but the more I do it, the better instincts I have about who to let into my life. Taking risks with people is essential for happiness. After all, it is better to have experienced at least some loving friendships than to sit alone, fearing heartache.

Let go of the old stories. I have let go of my mother. I realized that I was heading down a path similar to hers, and this taught me to feel compassion for her. I have released all the negativity that I held toward her, and now I just hope that one day she can learn to love herself. In order to let go, I needed to understand her. Because we were barely in contact, I had little information to go on. I collected everything I knew about her, from her childhood, her time with my dad, and the time she spent with me.

With all this information I recognized that my mother was a troubled woman who was unable to make real human connections. I sensed that she must have been suffering from some kind of depression or illness. By looking at her in this way, I could see that her leaving had nothing to do with me. Once I realized that our unhealthy non-relationship wasn't my fault, I was able to stop blaming her and hanging on to the victim story.

Once you stop telling the story, it has less power over you.

Choose not to hide from yourself. In the past, I tried to hurt and hide from myself, and all this did was make me lose myself further. By braving up and removing all the escape methods, I have found my raw being. Vulnerability is not a negative state. It is how we start our path. I have just started mine slightly later than most. By loving myself, I allow others to love me. I love myself because I am still here, and I can see my life changing around me. When I have moments of insecurity, I read through my journals, speak to friends, or throw myself into activities I enjoy, like baking.

Since changing my outlook, I have started working and have formed a number of great friendships. I have even gotten in touch with my mother and told her that I have forgiven her. I don't think we will ever have a relationship, but I am okay with that. The important thing is that I have finally opened myself up to other loving relationships. We can only do this when we make peace with our past.

CHANGING THE BELIEFS THAT KEEP YOU STUCK

by Sam Russell

> *Pain is inevitable. Suffering is optional.*
>
> —Unknown

I grew up believing that nothing I did was ever good enough, and this is something I still carry with me. It affects every aspect of my life: my hobbies, skills, relationships—even my understanding of my body, my appearance, and my mental health. I often think that I must have done something quite terrible in a past life to go through any of this, to not be good enough.

As certain as I've been of this, I've been sure that I wasn't responsible for these attitudes and beliefs. Other people did this to me, so I literally can't let go of the pain they caused. They hurt me too much—did too much damage for me to confront them, stand up to them, and forgive them. But blaming others hasn't helped me move on and become the person I want to be. It's helped me stay a victim, sure—and it's gotten me some sympathetic ears along the way—but it hasn't helped me get out of bed with a smile every morning for the past twenty-odd years. It's made me feel sluggish and sick to my stomach whenever the thoughts and memories worked their way into my consciousness.

There's no mystery to the way I think. Negative thinking is exactly that—negative. However, understanding negative thoughts is paramount to overcoming them. It's taken me a while to connect with the idea that the harmful actions of others has shaped my thinking; and it's taken me just as long to realize that it's time to let go. Change can come quickly, but more often it's a gradual process in which we endure and learn many lessons: I don't want to feel like this anymore, so I have to start changing my beliefs.

The first belief I'm changing: I'm a waste of time. Not true. I make a difference simply by being. I know I make a positive difference because I am mindful of my impact on the environment and do my best to reduce it. I support charities that are close to my heart with regular donations. My close friends wouldn't consider me a waste of time. Even though I sometimes find it difficult to believe, they do value my ideas and opinions, and they love my company.

The second belief I'm changing: Nothing I do is good enough. My ideas of perfection aren't mine—those ideas belong to other people. How can I ever live up to someone else's perfection? I can't. There are many things I can do with great success, but in order to make those achievements real for me, I have to define my own perfection: peanut butter on toast, growing my own fruit and vegetables, the smell of freshly baked vegan cookies, writing off the cuff and producing lucid prose.

The third belief I'm changing: I deserve pain. No, I don't. Nobody does. There's a difference between accepting responsibility for how you think about hurtful things other people have done, and taking the blame for those actions. I've not done anything to deserve the things that have happened to me.

And the last belief I'm changing: I'll never be happy. Not with that attitude, I won't—but then, aren't I already happy? I may not have all the things I want yet, like my dream job, but I do have a lot of other things in my life that mean a lot to me: my friends, my home, my cat, my family, waking up to the river every morning, my floating garden (I live on a boat), my creativity. Happiness comes from the small things— it comes from inside of me. I don't buy happiness or find it or receive it; I make it, for others and for myself.

The fact that people sometimes hurt other people won't change. My beliefs that have left me open to suffering—*my beliefs*—will change.

Take a minute to think of your beliefs about yourself. How many of these things are accurate? Which ones belong to you and to you alone? If you find a belief that you question, explore it and find out where it came from, what it's founded on. Challenge it. Become true to yourself. When you change your beliefs, you change your life.

It's taking time to work through these things, and I don't expect to be finished by next Monday, but that's what I love about change and self-improvement—there's no pressure to be complete tomorrow. I can do it all at my own pace, in a way that suits me. I'm a work in progress. And that gives me a lot of hope.

RELEASING SHAME AND LOVING ALL OF YOU

by Sarah Louise Byrne

> *When there is no enemy within, the enemies outside cannot hurt you.*
>
> —AFRICAN PROVERB

If you've had any experiences where you had to keep your truth quiet, particularly as a child, it's time to reclaim it and value its power. By doing so, you will release energy, old shame, and subconscious blocks that may now be holding you back from living your life to the fullest.

It could be that you had lots of family secrets (which creates shame), or it could be that you were bullied and felt unable to confide in anyone about it. There are many circumstances when we have our truth kept locked in. If you feel unable to speak your truth, then you feel shame. It's nature's law.

When we become shameful of our truth, we end up cutting off, discrediting, and devaluing a hugely important chunk of who we are and how we show up in the world. This is true for me. When I was growing up, my parents had an emotionally abusive relationship, and I was sworn to secrecy about it. My parents wanted no one outside of the house to know what was going on. While my father had anger issues, my mother always tried to keep the peace, so I decided it was better to not speak up or voice my feelings. Living under the same roof as them, it was impossible for me to not be affected by what was happening; yet I was unable to have my experience validated.

My parents were busy fighting, being in tension, or creating drama, and I was conditioned to not talk to anyone about our "trouble at home." So my truth was released only to my journal and me. After my parents divorced, I moved on to college and started my adult life. I felt proud of myself for staying strong through all the tough times at home, for being an emotional rock for my mother, and for forgiving my father for not being the kind of dad I wanted him to be. But in my mid- to late-twenties, things started to shift. After a few career U-turns, I started to feel unsure, confused, and shameful.

Up until that point I'd always considered myself to be strong, independent, and able to make decisions easily, and I was, overall, really confident. I wanted to understand where this shame came from. When in my life had I felt shame this strongly? It led me back to when I was unable to truly have presence as "me" growing up—I was the girl who could only be a silent participant in an unhealthy household. When I was told to not talk to anyone about what was going on, it was as if I was being told that my truth, perspective, and feelings were shameful.

At first I felt angry toward my parents and any adults who may have known what had been going on but hadn't shown concern toward my experience of the situation. But then, like a scientist, I detached and focused on how to release the shame. I could see that some part of me must still be carrying shame toward speaking my truth, and the only way to release it was to share it. So I told my story to a trusted friend (who is also a counselor). I made no omissions, and I quickly started to feel better. No one outside my family had known about what was going on, or what I'd experienced and seen. By telling someone outside of the family, I felt a shift—as if a spell was being broken.

Telling my truth did not make the sky fall down. It did not make me feel shameful. And it helped me see that while I'd been nurturing the brave, confident, no-BS side of me, there was a neglected side that needed to be seen—the lonely, frustrated, confused, and ignored side. Those "negative" aspects of ourselves are often the emotions we try to avoid, but as I began to validate them ("of course you felt isolated Sarah; the adults in your life were cutting you off from expressing yourself"), it helped me feel more compassion toward myself.

Feeling proud of yourself for your good qualities is one thing; being able to embrace yourself when you feel anger, resentment, or jealousy is another. And I learned that I have a right to feel all things. Just as it's okay to be excited, happy, and content, it's also okay to feel sad, nervous, and bored. Especially if you had an incident as a youngster where your "negative" emotions weren't given space to be expressed, it's important to be able to validate them now as an adult.

A lot of self-love work is about uncovering that hidden part of yourself and giving it light, room to breathe, and the capacity to exist. When we deny any part of ourselves, we are not allowing ourselves to be truly who we are. That's not to say we should broadcast all our vulnerabilities on Twitter or share intimate stories with people who we *know* are incapable of honoring our truth. It could mean seeing a counselor or airing it to a nonjudgmental support network.

When we realize we were "made" to keep our truths hidden by our environment or others, the first natural step is to feel angry, especially if this pattern of having to keep quiet took place as a kid or teen. Why didn't the adults in our lives do the right thing and give us space to be heard? Normally it had to do with their fears, insecurities, shame, and inability to face the truth for themselves. The important thing is to accept that they were *unable* to have done anything differently—to have provided you with what you needed.

Whatever you feel you needed (validation, support, safety to speak the truth), accept and make peace with the fact that you may never get these things from them. You can't rewrite history, and it may be likely that they are still, now, incapable of giving these things to you. What you can do today, right now, is begin to release the habit of self-repression that you may have learned from the past.

How do you do that? Start to shine light and love on your truth, whether that's turning your attention to your true passions that may have been ignored or taking baby steps to speak up on what doesn't work for you. Often we swallow our own opinions or needs in order to "keep the peace." It's time to take very small steps to rock the boat!

If you are subconsciously holding out for someone else to finally "see" you or love the real you, drop in with yourself and ask: "Do I see the 'real' me? Am I allowing my true self to be voiced, to be seen, to take up space?" Do you have spaces in your life where you can let your guard down and be authentic?

I've found that having my truths validated is hugely important, and this simple exercise is a good place to start: Visualize a kind, benevolent being (which could be a trusted friend or person you know, or your preferred idea of the universe/higher power/spirit) is with you, saying, "I love that you love." Then allow yourself to list all the things you love! Write down what you come up with.

"I love that you love making art. I love that you love dancing. I love that you love to have fun."

This always leaves me feeling reaffirmed and self-secure. It never fails to make me feel happy to be me. And it allows me to feel loved for who I truly am, not for what I do for others.

If you have repressed anger, frustration, or resentment (which is likely when we repress part of ourselves), find ways to healthily express it—for example, through a martial arts class.

Send love and validation to the aspects of yourself that perhaps your peers, family, and colleagues didn't or don't "get." You have to expand to be *all* of yourself.

FINDING BEAUTY IN YOUR SCARS

by Alexandra Heather Foss

> *Because of your smile, you make life more beautiful.*
> —THICH NHAT HANH

Beauty is a concept I struggle with—what it means, why it matters. I struggle because huge chunks of my life have not been beautiful. They have been ugly, marred by trauma, and accompanied by pain and anger.

We think of beauty and often visualize glossy magazine pages and wafer-thin models. We see beauty as superficial—eye color, hair texture, and numbers on a scale. We see beauty as something to be measured and weighed.

I don't see beauty that way. I see beauty as the grace point between what hurts and what heals, between the shadow of tragedy and the light of joy. I find beauty in my scars.

We all have scars, inside and out. We have freckles from sun exposure, emotional trigger points, broken bones, and broken hearts. However our scars manifest, we need not feel ashamed, but beautiful. It is beautiful to have lived, really lived, and to have the marks to prove it. It's a testament of our inner strength. To wear a snazzy outfit takes nothing; but to wear our scars like diamonds? Now that's beautiful.

Fifteen years ago, I would have laughed at this assertion. "Are you crazy?" I'd say, while applying lipstick before bed. I was that insecure. Lips stained, hair fried by a straightening iron, pores clogged by residue foundation, all in an attempt to be different from how I naturally was, to be beautiful for someone else. I hid my face because it hurt to look at myself in the mirror. I was afraid my unbeautiful truth would show somehow through my skin—that people would know I had been abused, and that in an effort to cope I was starving myself, harming myself. I was afraid people would see that I was clinging to life by a shredding thread.

Now? I see scars and I see stories. I see a being who has lived, who has depth, who is a survivor. Living is beautiful. Being a part of this world is beautiful, smile-worthy, despite the tears. Beauty isn't a hidden folder full of Kate Moss images for a kid who's dying to forget and fit in. And it isn't a fat-injected smile, or six-pack abs. It's the smile we are born with, the smile that sources from the divine inside, the smile that can endure, even if we've been through a lot.

My healing started with a birthday gift. It was a photograph my friend had taken of a forest, the word "forgive" painted in pink on a stone. I didn't understand why that word meant something until I really started to think about what forgiveness could mean. I'd blamed myself for so long for things that weren't my fault. Life stopped being beautiful to me, I stopped feeling beautiful inside, and my smile stopped shining beauty out into the world.

I think in order for us to make life beautiful we need to feel our smiles as we feel our frowns. For so long, I only honored my pain and my sorrow. I lost my smile, less because of the trauma and more because I spent so much time lamenting my scars. When I decided they were beautiful, I became beautiful. When I took power away from the negative emotions, my unchangeable traumatic past, I was better able to find joy in the present.

How did I do this? First, I made a soul collage, a board for the life of my dreams. I pasted onto the poster magazine images that depicted things I see as myself and want for myself. It became a beautiful visual guide for what matters to me beyond the superficial. This board reminds me to honor who I am in essence, who I was before anything bad happened to me, before I believed anything was wrong with me. This board provides me with a path of beauty through the scars.

Secondly, I found the book *The Why Café* by John P. Strelecky. In it, Strelecky encourages readers to pinpoint their PFE (purpose for existence). While reading, I realized beauty is my PFE. My purpose is to make whatever I can beautiful. Not beautiful in the superficial sense, but beautiful in the smile of the heart and soul sense. So far it's working.

Sometimes all it takes for your life to change is a shift in perspective. One solitary action, one solitary word, and everything is different. Take a moment now to smile. Do you feel it in your muscles? In your skin? In your toes? Where do you feel happiness?

When bad things happen we don't instinctively feel happy and beautiful, but we don't need to despair because life gets ugly sometimes. Joy and beauty are everywhere, in everything, in every one of us—no matter how we look, and no matter how we may hurt temporarily. Grace is beauty in motion, and we can create it by choosing to smile—to recognize that we're strong, despite our insecurities, and that the world is an amazing place, despite its tragedies.

We may hurt, but we will heal—and there is beauty in our scars.

Top 4 Tips About Moving Beyond Your Childhood Pain

1. **Tell empowering stories of healing in the present instead of sad stories of hurting from the past.**

    When you live in the story of how you were hurt, you define yourself by your pain, and you essentially pick up where others left off in mistreating you. It's hurtful and crippling to rehash these events over and over again (though it can be helpful in a therapeutic setting). When you find yourself dwelling on an old story, tell yourself that you're creating a new one—a story of forgiving and loving yourself in action. Try to understand whoever hurt you, and recognize that their actions were probably caused by their own pain. Then proactively choose to do something to take care of yourself in the way you wanted to be taken care of years ago.

2. **Challenge the limiting beliefs that make you feel bad about yourself.**

    You may be holding on to all kinds of limiting, inaccurate beliefs about your worth, your potential, and what you deserve. Realize these are not facts—you formed these beliefs based on difficult experiences and years of misguided thinking, and you can change your life by challenging these beliefs and forming healthier ones. When you start thinking the old belief, look for evidence to support the opposite one. It's there—proof of your intrinsic value is in your choices, your actions, and your daily life. You just have to start recognizing all the good you do.

3. **Shine a spotlight on your shame and douse it with empathy.**

When people abuse us, disrespect us, silence us, or disregard our feelings or needs, we often internalize that and feel shame, as if we deserved to be hurt because we were unworthy, bad, or flawed. We then feel the need to hide ourselves to avoid the pain of being seen, but hiding just creates more pain. It's not your fault that you feel shame—it's a natural response to the way you were treated—but it is your responsibility to heal it. Researcher Brené Brown wrote that shame requires secrecy, silence, and judgment to grow exponentially, and that it can't survive when doused with empathy. Offer yourself that empathy by choosing not to judge yourself for what other people did to you or what you did in response; and let someone else into that process, whether it's a friend or a professional.

4. **Recognize the beauty in your journey.**

You may not feel that all parts of you are beautiful, but there's beauty in the strength and courage that have helped you get where you are. Whatever you did in the past, you were doing the best you could, based on what you learned and experienced. Shift your focus and take some time to acknowledge how amazing your journey has been thus far. How have you displayed grace and bravery? How have all the chaotic dots of your past shaped up to create something unique and inspiring? If your life were a movie, what positive message would viewers take away?

CHAPTER 2

When You're Obsessed with Fixing Yourself: Realizing You're Not Broken

W E ' V E   A L L   F E L T   I T   I N   O N E   W A Y   O R   A N O T H E R — T H E   F E A R   T H A T there's something lacking in us. It might translate into a sense of worthlessness, as if we're frauds, flawed, or somehow damaged. It might be a less pervasive feeling, marked by the occasional suspicion we're not as good as people think we are. Or it might be an insecurity bubbling below the surface that we've yet to consciously acknowledge. Whether it's intense, slight, or even subconscious, we all experience this fear of being unworthy to some degree. If you do a Google search for the phrase "I'm not good enough," you'll find more than 69 million results.

Oftentimes, it's not just about self-judgment; it's about the foundational belief that we are somehow broken. It may seem like a natural conclusion when we struggle in ways we don't fully understand. Why am I still single? There's something wrong with me. Why do I take things personally? There's something wrong with me. Why do I keep making the same mistakes, or getting into the same unhealthy relationships, or doing the same things over and over and expecting different results? It's insanity, as Einstein said—or otherwise stated, there's something wrong with me.

We are the constant in all of our troubles, so we can easily blame ourselves every time we deal with something painful (which is not the same as taking responsibility). Or, we can convince ourselves that we wouldn't feel so bad if we could only fix ourselves. But the reality is we often suffer because we fight so hard against everything that hurts. We cause ourselves pain by telling ourselves we shouldn't be feeling it. And we become our own biggest problems by searching so desperately for solutions. We're not unhappy because we can't figure out how to change; it's because we sometimes tell ourselves that we can't be happy unless we do.

Perhaps the biggest challenge isn't learning how to repair ourselves, but rather learning to accept that we all deal with uncomfortable situations and emotions in life. We all have challenges. We all go through difficult times. We all deal with constantly changing and sometimes confusing feelings. And we all struggle to treat ourselves kindly every now and then. This doesn't make us damaged; it makes us human. At some point we need to decide that we're okay just as we are, even if we have room to grow.

How can we stop feeling unworthy? How can we challenge the beliefs that tell us there's something wrong with us? How can we stop trying to "fix" ourselves and instead embrace who we are in this moment? Countless Tiny Buddha contributors have addressed these questions on the site, sharing their experiences and insights. Some of those include . . .

ARE YOU RUNNING AWAY FROM YOURSELF?

by Amyra Mah

No matter where you go, there you are.

—CONFUCIUS

I am accustomed to not moving. To move was to feel pain—the pain of seeing how worthless I believed myself to be. Sometimes I would sit in the same place for hours, sometimes not leaving the house for days. By isolating myself, I avoided finding evidence in the outside world that proved how I saw myself was the absolute truth.

My worst nightmare was that others would show me (through what they said or didn't say, or what they did or didn't do) that they too found me as rotten as I knew myself to be. And so I was often left in the privacy of my own dreaded company. My best friends were the little pills I could rely on to knock me unconscious. I had neither the tolerance nor the strength to face myself, and I often chose the easy way out. Sedatives, tranquilizers, hypnotics—I lived for them. They provided me respite from the constant agony of my internal voice that asked, "What's wrong with me? Why am I so damaged? Why do I hate myself? What have I done to deserve this?"

Sleeping was my only escape. And I did more and more of it.

Sometimes I pushed the boundary too far—like the time when I swallowed enough hypnotics to probably kill a few buffalos. When I simply woke up a few hours later asking for coffee, I lost interest in testing myself that way again. But when I started realizing I was losing chunks of my memory, I knew I had reached my limit. I bumped into people on the street who talked about a party I had been at, and I had no memory of ever being there, nor the few days surrounding the event.

After that, I decided to go from one extreme to another, giving up sedatives in favor of stimulants—various amphetamine-based pills that would kick my body and mind into action so I could move, talk, and think at lightning speed. I figured if I kept moving, I wouldn't have to face myself. I was running away from the same problem, but I thought I'd found a better way of doing it. Stimulants helped me manage my social phobia. Whenever I went to a social event, I felt tremendous pressure to appear perfect. Every meeting, every interaction I had with people, was a performance. Drugs helped me feel more comfortable in my skin than I really was, but I felt false, and I hated myself for it.

I tried to exude confidence and charm. Many times, I succeeded. But always, I would spend the ensuing days beating myself up for every little incident I imagined had exposed the "rotten" me to the world. I began to feel the rage that had been suppressed for a long time. Somehow it didn't frighten me the way my other emotions did, so I took refuge in it. After suppressing my emotions for so long, I found it quite empowering to act out my aggression.

Acting out gave me a sense of power I'd never had. Now I can see that it's something I call "false power"—a false sense of power that's followed by feeling bad or dissatisfied because it comes from a place of fear. Soon, I was back to sleeping pills and began alternating them with the stimulants, one countering the aftereffects of the other. I was addicted to both not moving *and* moving too fast.

Then one day it occurred to me that maybe there was another place to look for the joys that had eluded me all those years. Whereas my options before were limited to the world I saw myself to be trapped in, somewhere in the middle, between not moving and moving too fast, there was a whole world of magical possibilities. I spent years trying to find easy access into this other world. I dabbled in a variety of spiritual practices—meditation, energy healing, and slower movements—but lacked the patience to persist when a door wasn't opened immediately. Yoga was too slow, Pilates too brutal, meditation too boring. I judged everything harshly. Some things were too wacky; others were not wacky enough. It reflected my mind, which had been swinging like a pendulum from one extreme to the other, struggling to come to a balance. But I did not give up. Slowly, I was finding beauty.

I learned that the other side of pain and false power is authentic power. Paradoxically, the place where I was to find the joys that had been missing was the very place I'd been running from all my life. When I reconnected to the parts of me that I had lost, it felt like a coming-home. I learned that self-love is when we come home to ourselves. That relationship which I had sought to destroy turned out to be the very thing that would save my life in the end.

What I realize now is that we can get so overwhelmed by our imperfections that we don't see any goodness in ourselves. In this way, we can destroy our relationship with ourselves, thinking we are flawed and beyond redemption. But it will only cut us off from the very source of joy, beauty, and love.

I see so many people addicted to substances and external relationships, believing that is where they can find joy and fulfillment. It will only feed into their deep inner insecurity and create more distance from themselves, the true source of joy. I see so many people either choosing to sleep through the everyday experience or run constantly from one place to the next, thinking they can escape their problem.

Freedom is found not by sleeping or running away, but by choosing to be awake and staying here long enough for the magic doors to open. The act of moving, mindfully, with an attitude of embracing life, will take you from feeling stuck with pain to healing it. Move slowly and you can taste the rich array of sensations. Move too quickly and you'll miss the gifts contained in the moment.

When you become vulnerable, feel emotions, and stay true to what you are feeling, you liberate yourself from pain. As you allow the sensations to be in your body, while gently breathing through it, you invite the natural force of change to renew you with its constant movement.

Through years of my own creation of movement therapy, I've cultivated a mindset of self-renewal. I am still discovering more and more goodness in me, and every discovery brings me even more joy. If you haven't found what you're looking for, try adjusting the pace with which you live your life and see if you can find that door to magical possibilities.

SEE LOVE AROUND YOU AND YOU'LL FEEL MORE LOVE WITHIN YOU

by Jennifer Chrisman

> *The most important thing in this world is to learn to give out love, and let it come in.*
>
> —Morrie Schwartz

There is a Native American tale that tells of a young boy speaking with his grandmother. She tells the boy that she has the spirit of two wolves living and battling inside of her. One is vengeful and unkind, as he sees all the world as a threat; the other is loving, secure, and nurturing. The little boy asks his grandmother, "Which one will end up winning?" and the grandmother replies, "Whichever one I feed."

We all have this pull inside of us. We can either nurture our fears and insecurities, or we can nurture our trust in love, kindness, and acceptance. This is not a new concept. There is an endless amount of information out there about connecting with your inner self and finding happiness from within—so much that it can feel overwhelming and even discouraging. If you're anything like me, you may find yourself still aching from a broken heart, or beating yourself up for the chocolate-chip cookie you just ate shortly after reading about finding forgiveness, gratitude, and self-love.

What I realized was missing in my quest for self-improvement—and what kept pulling me back to my old, familiar negative thinking—was faith. To make meaningful changes that allow us to release the grasp of our fears and limiting thoughts and beliefs, we have to be willing to believe in the positivity—*believe* that we deserve to stop beating ourselves up and looking for an external solution to "fix" us. It's not enough to just think it. We have to believe it.

The limiting beliefs of our fears are deep-rooted, so we need to meet them from our gut level. We need to really believe that it's okay to step out of our darkness and connect with our light instead.

Okay. So, how do we do that? We need to find evidence of that love around us. The world we see is a reflection of our inner experience. When we see love and light, we are connected to love and light inside of us. And conversely, when we see the inadequacies around us, we'll connect with that inside of ourselves.

Look around you. Where can you find evidence of the light in your life, the light within you? This concept was never more evident for me than when I had my son. Whenever my old, familiar, fearful thoughts creep up to tell me that I'm not good enough, that I don't have enough, or that everything is going to fall apart, then I think about him.

When I look at my son I'm able to clearly see the beauty and the purity of the human soul. He doesn't have to do anything to prove or earn his lovability; I certainly don't look at him and think, "Gee, if he lost a little weight, I'd love him more," or "When he meets that financial goal, that's when I'll love him." These thoughts don't even cross my mind when I think of him, so why would it seem logical to say them to myself?

We all started out in the same place, with a full capacity for love and loving. We weren't born into this world with fears of failure or being emotionally walled off. Children know no limitations until we point them out to them.

There was once a time in your life when your dreams knew no limitations, when you were free to take risks, and even if you fell down, you were able to get back up. That light is still in you. It doesn't ever go away; fear just overshadows it. Fortunately, fear is a learned response that has built up over time, which means that we can unlearn it!

When we allow ourselves to realize that the fear isn't real, we get to make a different choice. We can choose to find the love instead—to feed the loving wolf. I know that when I look at my son and I see that loving energy, it is *my* loving energy reflecting back at me.

Take a look around. Where do you see your loving reflection shining back at you? What inspires you? Where can you look for a reminder to stay connected to your belief that you deserve a life of love, and that the love and all possibilities are already inside of you? How can *you* stay present and aware of which wolf you are feeding?

ACCEPTING YOUR BATTLES: WHEN STRUGGLES BRING GIFTS

by Alison Hummel

> *It isn't what happens to us that causes us to suffer; it's what we say to ourselves about what happens.*
>
> —PEMA CHÖDRÖN

I love acceptance. Acts of surrender create forward momentum. If we all pause for a moment and observe what we are fighting, right here and right now—maybe depression, anxiety, weight gain, low self-image, or financial stress—we have an opportunity to accept. But that's just the start.

Recently I accepted something I never thought I would, and reframing the way I thought about it changed my life. I have moderate to severe obsessive-compulsive disorder (OCD). Having OCD is basically like believing everything that goes through your mind. Scary, right? Obsessive-compulsive people have intrusive and extremely terrifying thoughts—for example, that he may have been contaminated by something, which might lead him to spend hours washing. I have a base underlying all of my obsessions: that I will hurt people. It is my greatest fear.

I used to worry that I'd left the oven or iron on and that, in doing so, I may have burned the house down, which would ruin my husband's life and kill our cat. So I'd return home multiple times per day to check these appliances and also send my husband home to check. I also had massive rituals around shutting appliances off.

Obsessive-compulsives create rituals to lower the anxiety, which makes OCD a real time suck. I'd check to make sure I didn't leave the iron on, do everything evenly on both sides of my body so I felt "balanced," retrace events that happened in my life to make absolutely certain I hadn't harmed anyone accidentally, and search the Internet excessively for answers. These rituals literally took up hours of my day.

I discovered that I had OCD one afternoon when I was trying to figure out how you know something for certain. Try googling that. The first thing that popped up for my search query was about obsessive-compulsive disorder. I felt immediate relief. I leveraged my OCD to my advantage and feverishly searched the best treatment for this disorder. I discovered exposure response prevention (ERP). It's apparently the only game in town for this type of disorder, and luckily for me, Philadelphia houses one of the best treatment facilities in the world for OCD.

Once I completed the ERP, my OCD immediately went into remission. I was a diligent student, due mostly to how limited my life had become because of my anxiety. Because I didn't want to hurt anyone, I had no friends (I didn't want to hurt their feelings), my relationship with my husband suffered (I didn't want to hurt him), I spent hours on rituals to ensure that I hadn't hurt anyone, and I had lost about ten pounds in two and a half weeks when I hit my wall.

After the treatment, my anxiety lifted. I felt like a member of society for the first time in my life. But after about six months of freedom, something funny happened: I decided I didn't like having OCD anymore. I wanted that label off my back. But really, I didn't like the upkeep of remission.

Anxiety sucks, and ERP proposes that you habituate to the anxiety by just sitting with it. No deep breathing. No chemicals to relax the mind. Just straight-up anxiety. Anxiety naturally wears off. It's not possible for the human body to remain in an anxious state forever. And the human body is so amazing that we don't need to do anything to make it go away. But in order to get through the anxiety you must experience it. I didn't want to do that. I liked having my little rituals to deal with life.

So I un-accepted my limitation, just like that. The mind is a beautiful mechanism, really. I still find it so incredible that changing one's mind can have such wild repercussions. I decided to listen to my brain once again—to take the bait. I began fearing that I was a horrible employee, so I checked my email around the clock. I began believing that I was a bad wife and daughter, so the rituals around that came back with a vengeance. I began returning home to check on the iron.

Basically, most of the symptoms and rituals were back in full play and I had to go in for treatment again. In that second round, I made a resolution to myself that I will always accept that I have OCD. And it will most likely never go away.

I still cringed at the thought of having OCD. Let's face it, nobody wants to answer a series of questions from a shrink and then actually fit the profile of some well-known mental illness. But a mentor helped me see things differently. She suggested I look at my OCD as "cute" or "quirky."

"Cute?!" I yelped. You might have thought the woman suggested I run through Rittenhouse Square stark naked. I was appalled! But in that instant, something shifted. Her suggestion to look at a flaw as quirky was revolutionary. A good perspective. A new perspective. I began to refer to my OCD as one of my cute and quirky little additions to my personality. A nifty little surprise to the totality of my being. Something changed.

Now, my OCD is fully in remission, with no medications. This means I don't suffer severe anxiety at all anymore. I don't ritualize. I don't waste hours of my day checking on things. And most importantly, I rarely pay any attention to the thoughts that float through my beautifully complex brain.

Acceptance doesn't have to mean surrendering to bad news. In fact, accepting the bad part of anything can only take you so far. What if you began to look for the silver lining and accept that part? Let's say you struggle with depression. Studies show that people with depression may, and probably will, experience depression many times during their lives. So just getting out of the woods once is good, but it may come back again.

I think a lot of the time people get through something and say, "I will never go through that again." And when a smidge of depression creeps in, the person may try to run from it, and they begin to fear it, and they may try to "shake it off." This is a really negative way to deal with something. What if you said instead, "Oh, here we go. I see you. You are back. I can handle this."

Instead of running, welcome it back with open arms. It sort of deflates the whole thing. It's like a *whomp, whomp. . . .* When depression, anxiety, or whatever it is shows up again, can you see it as an old friend who needs a little TLC? Can you acknowledge that because of this struggle, you are able to experience many emotions that many other people cannot? Can you find the hidden benefits in your cross to bear?

I have this belief that people who have struggled with extreme lows can experience a deeper sense of joy than most people because they have known the depths of despair. Aron Ralston amputated his own arm in a hiking accident. He said he viewed the experience as a part of his life's purpose, part of his soul moving forward. Suddenly, accepting my OCD seems trivial (but still cute).

We can become so victimized by negative circumstances that we fail to see the gift that is right in front of us. As a writer, dreamer, and visionary, having this extra quirk can really add fuel to my fire. I am eager and ready for anyone who is done half-accepting or un-accepting something to join me in this new type of acceptance.

What limitation are you ready to flip on its head and accept—as a spice that just makes your soup taste that much richer?

WE DON'T ALWAYS HAVE TO BE HAPPY

by Jeanine Nicole

> *It is better to be whole than to be good.*
> —JOHN MIDDLETON MURRAY

Discouragement is usually an unwelcome guest. Every time it comes knocking on my door, I try to shoo it away or sweep it under the rug. In fact, many of us want nothing more than for happiness to be our constant state of being, and we have a hard time forgiving ourselves when we falter.

It happens: We can get immersed in the thick of discouragement for days, feeling mopey; downtrodden; physically, mentally, and emotionally "burnt out"; and all in all "not ourselves." When I am in this state, I avoid writing, interacting with others, and acknowledging my own feelings, all with the goal of not wanting to face the dark and shadowy sides of my own being. Though it doesn't always coincide with the external weather, I can feel rainy inside my own experience and mind from time to time, and I usually struggle against this feeling, making it worse.

I am adamant about being a positive person and believe that shining brightly is far preferable to feeling crummy. I think many of us share this tendency toward wanting to hold on to the light—but then, what do we do with our inner storms? Where do we get this notion that to be our truest and most beautiful selves we have to always be happy, elated, content, and sure of ourselves? Why do we believe that we must feel confident and inspired, have all the answers, and be buoyant in order to be our best, or at least to "be okay"?

We are only human after all, and nothing in our instruction manuals or in our description before we were born promises that we will always be perfect and shiny. And yet we carry this unrealistic pressure to be so and often berate ourselves for falling short any time a bad mood strikes.

It's tempting to only put our best foot forward. For example, on Facebook we can often share our sunshine-y moments proudly but may be less apt to proclaim as boldly when we are feeling negative. If not for wanting to hide our own seemingly fruitless negativity from others and even ourselves, we might also fear spreading the bad mood to others. We often forget that it actually gives others joy to be able to help, and it is often necessary to reach out, since "joy shared is doubled and grief shared is halved."

So how can you begin to admit or even embrace times when you may feel discouraged? In my life, I am beginning to acknowledge that it is just as natural to feel insecure, scared, and the need to curl up in bed in the fetal position as it is to feel peaceful, excited, or happy. I am even on my way to embracing all these states equally, and not trying to change my sadness or force it to be something it's not.

Sadness needs to be accepted. It needs to be loved, and cuddled, and caressed, and crooned: "It's okay, sadness. I see you. I love you. I respect and honor you, and I will let you be." It almost always feels a bit better just by being given the space to be allowed and received. Sometimes, as soon as I get on the phone with someone who cares, all the tears I didn't let myself cry start spilling out of me, because in simply being witnessed it is like the person actually reached out to give me the warmest hug.

It's important to appreciate ourselves similarly for all our aspects and to forgive ourselves for even the lowest facets of our self. Guilt, shame, self-flagellation—these don't actually correct the wrongs or make you a better person; they just reinforce the dark emotions even more strongly. So, instead of beating myself up, negating, or denying my sadness and grief, or trying to "fix" it, I simply repeat to myself the best words anyone ever told me: "Be gentle with yourself." Give yourself a big strong hug, maybe even a kiss, and tell yourself how much you appreciate you—*all* of you, now, in this moment, and forever.

Top 4 Tips to Stop Feeling Broken

1. **Identify what feelings you've been trying to numb or outrun.**

    To name a thing is to have power over it. Get clear about any beliefs or feelings you've been numbing with food, alcohol, drugs, or any other quick fix. What is it that you're trying to escape, and why? What mistakes are you still judging, what flaws are you condemning, what experiences are you trying to forget? There's nothing wrong with you for having these feelings; it only feels wrong because you're avoiding them instead of growing through them. Once you understand your emotions, you can challenge yourself to sit with them, learn from them, and let them go. It might be uncomfortable to feel what you've avoided, but the only way out is through.

2. **Talk to yourself as you would a sibling or friend.**

    Think about someone you love and all the positive qualities you believe they possess. Now consider that, just like you, they are human and flawed. When you're tempted to berate yourself for a mistake or perceived weakness, talk to yourself as if you were that person. You likely wouldn't consider them broken, but you'd consider them unique and worthwhile. You wouldn't talk to them with disdain or judgment, but you'd comfort them with understanding and compassion. Talk to yourself as you'd talk to them—and as they would talk to you.

3. See the gifts in your challenges.

Think about all the things you've tried to change or fix—everything you've used as evidence to believe or prove that you're not worthy. Now identify how these things have somehow helped you or other people. For example, if you experience strong emotions, does this passion translate into your work? This doesn't mean you can't strive to improve; it just means you see yourself as the totality of darkness and light—just like everyone else—and recognize that you have immeasurable value, exactly as you are now.

4. Realize that feeling the full range of emotions is not something you have to "fix."

We often think of happiness as a destination—an enduring positive feeling we hope to know someday. Then when we struggle or experience a setback, we assume that something's wrong—with us, or with life in general. Consider instead that it's normal to experience highs and lows—that this is a natural part of life. If you're going through a hard time, instead of making it worse by getting down on yourself, tell yourself, "It's okay to be where I am right now. I know I won't feel this way forever, and I'll feel better sooner if I accept this moment instead of judging myself for living it."

CHAPTER 3

When You Focus on Your Flaws: Accepting All of You

IF YOU LOOK FOR THINGS TO IMPROVE IN YOURSELF, YOU WILL likely find an infinite list of things that you could change. You'll find physical features to alter, weaknesses to confront, and bad habits to eliminate. If you address them, you'll likely find new flaws to fix, new shortcomings to address, and new inadequacies to mitigate. You can spend your whole life condemning yourself for everything you're not, and never run out of reasons to feel down on yourself for not being perfect. You might even convince yourself that the world puts this pressure on you—that it's your parents' fault, or society's fault, or the media's fault—and you wouldn't be entirely off base in recognizing that our culture exploits our fear of being flawed.

In a world where change sells, and sells well, we can easily find a million and one products to address our various imperfections. So we buy creams and gels and lotions and pills. We take courses and seminars and webinars and workshops. And we hire coaches and trainers and mentors and guides. Yet we still find ourselves struggling with a sense of lack, which further fuels our compulsion to buy. The weight loss industry brings in billions each year while obesity rates steadily increase. The self-improvement industry grows by leaps and bounds while antidepressant use skyrockets. Despite our best efforts to better ourselves—or maybe because of them—we find ourselves feeling overwhelmed by everything we just can't fix.

We then stock up on reading material that helps us learn to accept ourselves (books like this one included), and we try to reconcile the unhealthy desire to attain perfection with the healthy desire to grow and improve. We don't want to buy into the idea that we're defective, but we also don't want to stagnate. We don't want to convince ourselves that we're inferior, but we also don't want to limit our ability to reach our full potential. And we don't want to hinge our sense of self-worth on other people's approval, but oftentimes we know no other way to gain our own.

Our culture may feed into our fears of inferiority, but we're the ones who need to be responsible for what we think, believe, and do. We can see ourselves as the simple sum of all our challenges and weaknesses, or as the complex culmination of both the dark and the light.

How do we start appreciating our complexity? How can we start valuing our imperfect selves as the people who love us do? How can we feel more comfortable in our own skin, with less judgment and more understanding and compassion? Countless Tiny Buddha contributors have addressed these issues on the site, sharing their experiences and insights. Some of those include . . .

OVERCOMING PERFECTIONISM IN A CULTURE THAT PROMOTES IT

by Lucy H. Pearce

> *Good enough is the new perfect.*
>
> —BECKY BEAUPRE GILLESPIE AND
> HOLLEE SCHWARTZ TEMPLE

I stand accused of being a perfectionist. My plea? Not guilty, of course! "I'm not perfect enough to be a perfectionist!" I counter. But the evidence is stacked against me. Ladies and gentlemen of the jury, Exhibit A: my first year at university, our midterm examination in literature. There was major building work going on outside, and concentration was nigh on impossible. As a result, our tutor added 10 percent onto everyone's scores to make up for the disruption. What did I get? One hundred and ten percent. And what was my first thought? "Hmm, I could've done better. And anyway, it was so easy."

Out of the 140 other kids in the class, how many others got 110 percent? You guessed it—it was just me. This is it, you see, the madness of perfection: it isn't even satisfied with perfection.

Another example: a couple years later, I planned, cooked for, and led the ceremony for my own wedding. The day went smoothly.

Many people said it was the most special, personal wedding they had ever attended. But I felt disappointed, in floods of tears at the minor imperfections, which no one but me had noticed. And despite having lost thirty pounds and being on the verge of being underweight, I still felt fat.

What is tragic is that I know I am not alone in this.

I had been hypnotized by the madness of the perfection-focused culture we inhabit, where even the most beautiful of bodies are airbrushed, and talented voices are digitally enhanced to reach ever-new heights of perfection. We are shown the sublime, and have been acculturated to search for the flaw. No wonder we always feel ourselves falling short.

It seems that everything is now within the sphere of the perfection virus, not just our school test scores, but our bodies, our homes, our weddings, our parenting, our intimate relationships. We are expected, according to conventional "wisdom," to "give 110 percent"—all the time. "Failure is not an option," we are chided. "You can always do better, be happier, be richer, look younger . . ." I bet you recognize this?

Even those of us who like to believe that we perch outside this mainstream hysteria are often pulled in by the books of self-help gurus and spiritual guides demanding that we be more mindful, more patient, richer, less worldly. Everywhere the message is the same: You are not good enough the way you are. You. Must. Try. Harder.

We buy this, right? We take these messages into our hearts and stab ourselves in the back with them every day. But at some point every perfectionist discovers that even 110 percent isn't enough. We find ourselves trapped in the perfection spiral: creatively blocked, self-loathing, controlling, and alone. And we see that perfection is not an absolute, but always shifting, unreachable, indefinable—and outside our grasp.

Perfectionism is our denial of two very basic truths of existence: we are not perfect; and we are not, ultimately, in control. When we absorb the law of perfection, we are infected with the virus of self-doubt, which eats away at every area of our lives. The more perfect we are, we believe, the more valid we are as people. But with every advance in one area, we find ourselves wanting in another. We worry that we are not good enough, and, therefore, on some level that we do not deserve love, happiness, or maybe even life itself.

We fear our imperfections will expose us as failures when actually they show the places we have grown, the markers of our realizations, our unique situation in the sands of time and cycles of nature. In the words of Leonard Cohen, "There is a crack in everything. That's how the light gets in."

The truth of the matter is that in our quest for perfection, we negate our experiences and ourselves. In a perfect world, in a perfect story, the moment of 110 percent would have been the perfect lesson. So neat and tidy. But in reality it took many more years of hating my beautiful body, being bridezilla over my special wedding, and finally being simply a good enough mother with my three imperfect children to lead me to this moment (which I still have to relearn continuously): I will never be perfect. I can only be good enough.

Having seen the impossibility of perfection, I sought another path, another gauge—one that has become popular in recent years: the 80/20 rule. This states that for any project or endeavor we take on we need to focus on the first 80 percent, because the final 20 percent takes 80 percent of the effort. 80 percent is good enough. And it's usually the last 20 percent that exhausts us and kills our creativity. This rule requires the "good girl" or "good boy" in us to settle for 80 percent. For the overachiever, it can feel, at first, like going out in your underwear.

But soon you notice more joy in your work, more freedom to experiment, take risks, make mistakes. And most of all you notice that you are getting more of you—your work, your love, your voice, out into the world, rather than withholding it for fear it is not good enough.

Jason McLennan in his wonderful book *Zugunruhe* talks about the theory of ¾ baked: "When I talk about ideas or tasks being ¾ baked, I mean that they have reached a special moment in time or development where the idea has significant shape . . . that it can be offered up, in its stage of near completion." He continues by explaining that when we release our work at this stage, it means that others can help us to hone and polish our creations, which makes the end result far more powerful than the work of one mind can ever be.

Learning to drop an extra 5 percent is another place for learning. It requires us to release our need to define ourselves by our work, for its perfection to be a reflection of our own ego, and instead allow collaboration and feedback to be part of creativity. It makes us let go of our need to be in control. This is what I aim for now: no longer perfection, but a glorious work in progress. A living creation—be it myself or any project or relationship I have—which is always evolving and changing, with feedback and input not only from myself, but everyone around me.

And so I am, rather imperfectly, learning to embrace my own imperfections—the glorious typo that escapes my final edit; my gray hairs; my stretch marks; the freckles on my nose; my moments of impatience and forgetfulness; the mess in the kitchen; the way I get oversensitive when I socialize too much . . .

These are the signs that, for today, I am choosing to live with compassion for myself—and, by extension, for others; that I am embodying the dynamism of life itself rather than control or blocking its flow. Knowing that truly, on every level, I am good enough. And so are you.

THE KEY TO BEAUTY AND ACCEPTANCE IS YOU

by Jaclyn Witt

> *To be beautiful means to be yourself. You don't need to be accepted by others. You need to accept yourself.*
>
> —THICH NHAT HANH

I read the quote above from Thich Nhat Hanh the other day, and I have to say, nothing has shaken me to the core more.

I was diagnosed with a rare form of muscular dystrophy at the age of two, and growing up I always struggled with loving myself and having self-confidence. For the most part, you wouldn't know I have a serious physical disability aside from my visible limp, my difficulty getting up and down stairs, and my tendency to fall when I get weak.

I was never able to do sports growing up like my friends and often had to enroll in special adaptive Phys. Ed. classes in school. I always felt my disability separated me from my peers, so I put up an emotional wall and convinced myself that I had to wear the latest clothes, have perfect skin, and have the perfect body in order to "blend in" with everyone around me—in order to be truly loved. Then maybe I would be considered beautiful. Then maybe no one would notice I was different.

If I just looked like those Victoria's Secret models, then someone would accept and love me. So often we look to external things to define our beauty, most commonly, our physical appearance. We think that if we just fit into the mold that society has told us is "good-looking" then we'll feel good about ourselves and will gain acceptance.

I put a lot of value in being in a relationship too. Because of my disability, I was extremely shy for a long time and very insecure. All I wanted was for a guy to come along, sweep me off my feet, and fall in love with me. Then I thought I would truly be like everyone else, because I would have someone (other than friends and family) there all the time telling me that I was loved and valued.

In today's world especially, it's hard not to feel like our lives need to have a certain set of circumstances for us to truly be accepted. With social media like Facebook, we're exposed to all the intimate details of a lot of people's lives at one time. When they get engaged, married, have children, or are traveling the world with their fabulous jobs, we know almost instantly. For a lot of us, that creates increasing internal pressure to have our life be a certain way because we think that's what we need to feel happy with ourselves and be accepted in the world. We look to all of these other things outside ourselves to feel beautiful and to feel accepted when the whole time the only person who can truly allow us to feel these things is staring back at us in the mirror every day.

After I read the Thich Nhat Hanh quote about beauty, I went to clean the bathroom in my house and was suddenly overcome with emotion. I realized that all those things I'd been doing were what I thought I needed to do for everyone else to accept me, when in reality I wasn't accepting myself. Whether it was having a boyfriend, having a lot of friends, or looking "perfect" all the time, I was trying to show everyone else, "Hey! Look! Someone loves me! I have value now!"

Really though, *I* was the one who didn't like that I was different. I was the one who couldn't accept this disease I was born with. I had amazing friends and an incredibly supportive family who didn't care if I walked with a limp or not—people who didn't care that I couldn't run a marathon or that sometimes I needed their help getting up a curb. I was even told growing up how beautiful I was, but I couldn't understand why I never felt like it. It's because I wasn't truly being myself and accepting myself. I didn't feel beautiful, and no amount of people telling me I was beautiful was going to change that. I was letting a circumstance I was born with define me and define how I thought others saw me.

In our extremely visual culture, I think we all struggle with the idea of "beautiful." And it can feel like no one ever really says, "Just be yourself, love yourself, and accept yourself. *That* is true beauty." Beautiful doesn't mean being physically attractive or looking like those people we see on TV or in magazines. It's not defined by having or not having a significant other or by how many friends we have. We're all born with our own struggles, and beautiful isn't defined by those either. Beautiful means just being and loving you!

I wasted many years trying to do everything I could to be considered beautiful by my peers and by society. Comparing myself to others and wondering why my life wasn't like this or that. The thing we don't realize is that we are beautiful all along just by being ourselves. And *we* are the key to accepting ourselves—no one else. There's only one of each of us, and this is our chance to really live, so why waste our energy trying to gain acceptance from everyone around us and trying to make ourselves look perfect in order to feel loved?

When you start down that road to self-acceptance—that road to truly loving who you are, flaws and all—you can truly open yourself up to being beautiful, for you and no one else.

FEELING COMFORTABLE IN YOUR OWN SKIN

by Mary Dunlop

The moment you accept yourself you become beautiful.

—OSHO

From the time I was a little girl, people told me I was pretty, but I never believed them. Instead, I scrutinized myself in the mirror searching for ways to look better, not realizing that what I was really looking for was a way to be me and feel good about myself. As I focused even more on my looks throughout my twenties, I became increasingly self-conscious and dependent on how others perceived me. If someone complimented me and gave me attention, I would feel confident. But if I went unflattered or unnoticed, I would return to the mirror in an effort to figure out why.

I had often heard the expression "what you are inside shows on your face." However, I didn't know what these words truly meant until one day at the age of thirty-five. That day, I took another long look in the mirror, and suddenly something clicked: My looks were not the problem—they never were.

Somehow I understood that what I didn't like about my face had nothing to do with my physical features. It was something else;

something within myself that was reflecting out and causing me to feel unattractive, ill at ease, and unconfident. At that moment, I knew there were two things I needed to do. The first was to stop staring in the mirror. The second was to look at what was going on inside.

Soon, a friend recommended meditation, so I gave that a try. I sat, breathed, quieted my thoughts, and shared my feelings in a nine-hour course, which I soon followed with a two-day silent meditation retreat. It's possible that a silent retreat may not be for everyone, but it was one of the most valuable experiences of my life. The two days forced me to reflect and be with myself in an environment that did not permit social interaction, not even eye contact. There were also no distractions, such as telephone, TV, books, or computers.

Was the experience disagreeable? Initially, yes. Was it painful? Sometimes. But it allowed me to bring forth a lot of valuable self-information and one remarkable realization: I became conscious of how unnatural I felt. In the time I was there, I recognized that I was not uncomfortable in that setting because I didn't know how to be with myself. I was uncomfortable because I didn't know how to *be* myself.

This was also why I often felt unattractive and ill at ease with others. I was frequently projecting someone who didn't feel like me, and that projection habitually depended on who I was interacting with. It was this realization that launched my journey to authenticity and the discovery of a beautiful me. Slowly, I started to learn about myself and the things that make me happy, and I found that I had a rhythm. I could hardly believe it, but I actually had my own beautiful flow, and as soon as I began to follow it, my authenticity started to build on itself.

I gradually began to feel less self-conscious around others and much more comfortable with myself. For the first time in my life I started to feel well and beautiful—and it showed. I saw it in the mirror. My husband noticed it in my body language. He said I carried myself differently, like I had more confidence and ease.

If you're looking for ways to feel more at ease with yourself, start by honoring your body. I can't say enough on how important it is to celebrate your body. Every day I thank my body for all that it does, and I honor its needs through thirty- or forty-minute runs, long showers, flossing my teeth, and drinking lots of water.

It helps to make a list of the things you need to do to take care of yourself so you feel healthy and grounded. Then, schedule them into your day. It's easier to feel good about who you are when you make your needs priorities.

Along with running, creative writing has contributed greatly to my journey. It keeps my mind filled with positive thoughts, and so much of who I am comes out in the characters I write about. I also love to read, learn new things, and travel to different places, even if it's just to new areas or neighborhoods near my home. Doing what you love is an important step in loving who you are. What practices make you feel passionate and positive about the way you're living your life?

Lastly, make an effort to maintain a healthy, happy spirit. Without inner peace, authenticity is fleeting. I meditate daily and do my best to live where peace is found—in the present moment. I also make a point of watching one or two funny movies every week. Nothing helps my spirit soar as much as laughter. It helps me see the world through younger eyes and reminds me that, no matter what, every moment contains hope and possibilities.

Take time out to nurture your spirit, whether that means practicing yoga, walking on the beach, or simply relaxing. In order to be comfortable with yourself, you first need to be comfortable just being. And always keep in mind that finding your authenticity—finding yourself—*will* help you feel your beauty. When you endeavor to be who you are and be true to yourself, you will automatically feel attractive and unique.

TRANSFORMING JUDGMENTS INTO ACCEPTANCE, FOR OTHERS AND OURSELVES

by Jarl Forsman

> *If we learn to open our hearts, anyone, including the people who drive us crazy, can be our teacher.*
>
> —PEMA CHÖDRÖN

Every person you meet has something special to give you—that is, if you are open to receiving it. Each encounter offers you the gift of greater self-awareness by illustrating what you do and don't accept about yourself. An honest look will show you that the reactions you have to others give you more information about yourself than about them. You can never know for sure what motivates other people, but you can learn what you are accepting or judging in yourself.

For instance, if someone makes a remark about you, and it's something you also judge in yourself, it will most likely hurt. However, if they make the same remark and you *don't* have that judgment about yourself, it probably won't bother you at all.

I remember an experience that now seems almost insignificant but at the time really hurt my feelings. I was scheduled to go to a special party and I didn't feel I had the right item of clothing to complete my outfit.

I didn't have the money to go out and buy something new, and I was a little distraught. I was walking home, preoccupied by this wardrobe dilemma, when I happened upon a box of clothes for people in the neighborhood marked "free." I don't usually look in free boxes, but this time, for some reason, I did. I took a peek inside and lo and behold, I found the *perfect* top to complement my outfit. Not only was I excited about the outfit but I felt like I had experienced some serious magic. I told a few friends at the party what had happened that day because I thought it was proof positive of the synchronicities occurring in the universe that we are rarely aware of.

I was at an event later that month when one of my friends who had been at the previous party walked up to me and said, "Oh, you're wearing *that* old thing?" Now, had I simply been grateful for the fortuitous (and free) gift that I'd received, which perfectly fulfilled my couture conundrum, I probably wouldn't have had the slightest reaction. I would have felt happy and lucky. But when she said those words, I felt like I'd been stabbed. I immediately felt self-conscious and less-than, embarrassed and a little ashamed. And the reason I felt this way was because I had judged myself for not being able to buy a new top and wearing a scavenged piece of clothing. If I had not had that judgment of myself, her words would have simply rolled right off me like water off a duck's back.

Our reactions always have more to do with our own self-judgments and feelings of inadequacy or strength, than what the other person may say or do. Most judgments we make about others stem from one of these basic causes:

You wouldn't tolerate the same behavior or characteristic in yourself. For instance, you might be shy and encounter a very gregarious person. Your judgment might go something like this: *What a show-off. They are so loud and obnoxious.* Because you would be embarrassed to act this way, you resent somebody else doing it. This type of judgment might reveal that you are not fully expressing yourself, hence you feel resentful or put off by others doing so, even if they do it clumsily. Becoming aware of the truth of this reaction and working on expressing yourself more fully and authentically would result in a valuable gift of freer self-expression.

You display the same behavior and aren't aware of it, so you project your disowned behavior onto others and dislike it "out there." Everyone has encountered this at some point. Someone is complaining about a friend or acquaintance and you think to yourself, "That's funny, they do the very same thing they're complaining about!" Take an honest look within to see if you share some of the characteristics you dislike in others. You may be surprised to learn that you do. This discovery can offer valuable insight and help you gain greater self-acceptance and compassion for others.

You are envious and resent the feelings that come up, so you find something wrong with those who have what you want and end up judging them. Someone who has attained recognition in some area may remind you of your own lack of success by comparison. You may resent their higher degree of accomplishment and then find something wrong with them in order to avoid your own feelings of inadequacy. Since inspiration is a much more effective motivator than competition, you'd be more likely to experience success if you got inspired by other people's victories instead of wasting time finding fault with them.

Most judgments of others are ego strategies to avoid uncomfortable feelings. However, if you lack the awareness of where they come from, they can lead to even more discomfort down the line. Becoming aware of the nature of your judgments doesn't mean that you no longer have preferences. You may still notice that certain types of behavior seem unappealing. But with the right understanding and a little personal work, discernment rather than judgment kicks in and causes you to feel compassion for others, even if you're not enthusiastic about their behavior. At the very least, you'll feel neutral.

Discernment is awareness and understanding without an emotional response. Exercising discernment feels very different from getting your buttons pushed. Judgments that cause emotional reactions are clues to help you find personal insight.

When you explore your beliefs and assumptions instead of judging people, you open a door to expanded self-awareness and self-acceptance. Rather than unconsciously delighting in the ego gratification of judging others, you let your reactions and judgments help you achieve greater self-understanding—and accordingly, greater happiness and success.

When you use your judgment of others as a mirror to show you the workings of your own mind, every person's reflection can become a valuable gift, making each person you encounter a teacher and a blessing.

Top 4 Tips About Self-Acceptance

1. See yourself as a work in progress.

When you focus on perfection, you inevitably feel dissatisfied because perfection is unattainable. Shift your focus instead to lifelong growth, and recognize that we are all works in progress, constantly evolving and never finished. From this space, you're better able to see challenges and setbacks as a valuable part of the journey—which is in itself the destination—rather than an obstacle to where you want to be.

2. Accept yourself in action (and model it for others).

Oftentimes when we don't accept ourselves, we look outward for acceptance; but in actuality, it needs to happen the other way around. We teach people how to treat us through our actions. Teach people to accept you for exactly who you are by showing them what that looks like: Celebrate your positive qualities; talk to yourself kindly and make self-care a priority; reinforce that you're doing the best you can, and your best is good enough; and recognize that your poorest choices don't define you.

3. **Create stillness to feel more at ease with yourself.**

When we refuse to accept ourselves, there's a feeling of resistance—this sense of fighting who we are and trying to escape or transform it. We naturally feel uncomfortable when we refuse to let ourselves be ourselves. Take time to simply be, whether that's through yoga, meditation, or deep breathing. From this place of mental stillness, it will be easier to recognize and honor your authentic self—and enjoy all the things that make you feel happy, passionate, and fulfilled. When you grow into yourself, acceptance is a natural consequence.

4. **Use your judgments as a mirror to grow into greater self-acceptance.**

Recognize what behaviors you judge in others and use them as a compass to understand where you need to offer yourself compassion, and where you may want to challenge yourself. If you judge people who seem needy, are you ashamed of holding that quality? Can you offer yourself compassion for that trait, and in doing so, start understanding and transforming it? If you judge people who go for their dreams, is there a part of you that is holding yourself back? Can you push yourself out of your comfort zone in some way, which will make you feel proud of yourself?

CHAPTER 4

When You're Hard on Yourself: Embracing Self-Forgiveness

WHEN WE'RE KNEE-DEEP IN THE MESSY CONSEQUENCES OF A choice we wish we didn't make, it can be challenging to remember that mistakes are crucial for growth. Sure, we may know this, in much the same way we know that losses often lead to gains, and that it's sometimes a blessing to not get what we want. But when we don't yet see the gain, the blessing, or the lesson, it's not quite as easy to forgive ourselves and feel peace.

We can end up berating ourselves, judging not only our decision but also our character, as if we *are* our worst mistakes. It's a dark, lonely road to tread, and yet we so frequently choose to walk it. We dwell on everything we think we did wrong and wonder what it means about us that we made those decisions: A good person would never have behaved so irrationally. A strong person would never have reacted so emotionally. A wise person would never have responded so aggressively. Then, armed with all this proof that we're not good, strong, or wise, we can end up feeling ashamed, depressed, and helpless—as if the horrible feeling of this moment will endure, and perhaps we will deserve it.

We then start grasping for some sense of control with thoughts of "what if" and "if only"—as if dwelling on everything we should have done can somehow change what's passed and what's coming. Of course, this regret and self-flagellation never makes a bad situation better; if anything, it compounds it, since it keeps us stuck trying to change yesterday to the detriment of the today.

But it's not only our poorest decisions that we allow to cause us grief and stress. Sometimes we blame ourselves for things we didn't do, or couldn't do, or perhaps didn't know to do—the times we didn't speak up, the people we couldn't protect, or the friends we never knew to help. We expect a lot from ourselves, and we can easily get down on ourselves if we feel we've fallen short or somehow let others down.

If you've never beaten yourself up in this way, then you've grasped what it means to truly forgive yourself and move forward a little stronger from each misstep or challenge. If this all sounds familiar to you, then you may need some help reframing your response to mistakes, allowing yourself to learn from them, and then forgiving yourself so you can move on. Countless Tiny Buddha contributors have addressed these issues on the site, sharing their experiences and insights. Some of those include . . .

FORGIVING YOURSELF WHEN YOU HURT SOMEONE ELSE

by Michael Davidson

> *Be gentle first with yourself if you wish to be gentle with others.*
> —LAMA YESHE

Think back to the last time somebody apologized to you about something. Did you forgive them? There is a very good chance that you did. Now think back to the last time you harmed someone else. Have you forgiven yourself? Probably not.

We all make mistakes. Oftentimes, through our actions, somebody gets hurt.

During this past year, I served as a liaison between my fraternity and a seventeen-year-old cancer patient in a local hospital through the Adopt-A-Family program. The patient, Josh Goldstein, passed away around the beginning of March. (I'm not exactly sure when.) My responsibility as liaison was to have a regular communication with Josh. I failed in this responsibility.

In the month after Josh died, I felt overcome by shame. My belief that I was a fundamentally good person was shattered. How could I be so neglectful? Why did I not spend more time with Josh? This feeling climaxed during Family Hour of Rutgers' University Dance Marathon (a thirty-two-hour, student-run event that raised money for families that have children with cancer and blood disorders). I was standing in the rafters listening to a speech by the mother of one of the families we had helped. I couldn't bear to hear her thank us for all the wonderful things she said we had done when I felt deep down that *I was a bad person!* I literally could not touch my friends, who were standing next to me, because I might have contaminated them with the disease that was my poor character.

This terrible feeling continued, and tears began to stream down my face. Flashing before my eyes, I saw all the opportunities I had to visit Josh in the hospital but had chosen not to. Then my memory came to our fraternity meeting where Josh's death had been announced. His last wish had been that we would not forget him after he passed. I pictured Josh saying this over and over again.

And then a strange thing happened. I realized that not only was I not going to forget Josh, but that I would never make the same mistake again. In an instant, I had forgiven myself, let go of the pain, and accepted that I could still be a good person even though I had made a serious mistake.

I've learned a few things about self-forgiveness. One is that, despite our flaws, we are okay, just as we are. Your flaws, rather than making you "less" of a person, are what make you, *you*. What you think of as a defect actually makes you far more interesting to others. You are not perfect. You make mistakes. But you are also on a path of growth. Your mistakes and failures help you improve. As flawed as you may be, you must accept yourself, flaws and all, if you are to make progress in your life.

You can do something wrong while still being a good person. A lot of guilt or shame can make you feel like there is something wrong with you. Realize, right now, that there is a very big difference between *doing* a bad *thing* and *being* a bad *person*. Even when you do something that you regret, you had a valid reason for doing it at the time (even if that reason doesn't make rational sense). You didn't do something bad because you are a fundamentally bad person; there was an intent, or valid motivation, behind your action.

If you are struggling with guilt, it might help to talk to someone about what happened. Sometimes you just need to get it off your chest. Talking to someone else about what is bothering you can have serious benefits. For one, it provides another perspective. When you are upset with yourself, emotions can cloud your reasoning abilities. A friend will often point out a reason you deserve to forgive yourself that you never would have seen. Secondly, it will likely make you feel better to realize someone else has your back. Knowing that other people are not as critical of you as you are of yourself can be encouraging.

If your internal voice is getting overly cruel, it can be helpful to "personalize" it. Imagine that there is some other entity that is thinking your self-critical thoughts, and have a conversation with them. It might sound silly, but you should give this entity a name, which will reinforce the idea that this voice is separate from you. During your "conversation," ask your internal, critical voice what their positive intention is. This voice is saying what it is saying for a reason. It might be to protect you, to prevent you from making the same mistake again, or to help you improve in some way.

When you realize that your thoughts of guilt or shame are intended for your benefit, it becomes easier to forgive yourself. You can find another way to satisfy that positive intent while reducing your guilty feelings. In my case, one of the positive intentions of my internal voice constantly shaming me was to help me remember Josh after he passed. Since forgiving myself, I have dedicated each of my yoga sessions to Josh, which ensures that he will not be forgotten.

If you still feel unable to forgive yourself, imagine your best friend did exactly what you did and has now come to you for advice. What would you tell them? You would reassure them and tell them not to be so hard on themselves. You would tell them that everyone makes mistakes. You would tell them that they deserve to be forgiven. Why can't you say this to yourself?

Forgiving yourself is far more challenging than forgiving someone else because you must live with yourself and your thoughts 24/7. Despite the challenge, an emotionally healthy person must have the capacity to forgive themselves when they have made a mistake. When you forgive yourself, you are not pretending as though it never happened. On the contrary, you are acknowledging that your actions have consequences. But the consequences need not include self-inflicted negative feelings.

Not forgiving yourself is like picking at an open wound; you are only making a bad situation worse. The wound is already there, but you have control over your reaction to it, and you can stop it from getting worse. If you can forgive yourself when you make a mistake, it becomes easier to address the consequences of your actions in a productive way.

THIS MOMENT DOES NOT DEFINE YOU

by Lisa Stefany

> *Things and conditions can give you pleasure but they cannot give you joy—joy arises from within.*
>
> —ECKHART TOLLE

I struggled with anorexia for four years before I went to rehab. Rehab saved my life, and although I am not "completely recovered," I am *in recovery.* I am coping. I am living again.

One of the biggest sources of fuel for my eating disorder was my hyperfocus on the physical and transitory aspects of life. In my mind, I overemphasized the importance of my body. I put the appearance of my body, and how I felt about my body, above my true, underlying nature. I would treat fleeting thoughts, feelings, and emotions as crucial, life-and-death matters. I did not realize or appreciate my enduring self, which (I now understand) transcends the fleeting states of the corporal realm.

When I was anorexic, surface feelings took on a villainous and critical role. I know this sounds melodramatic and unrealistic (because it is), but "feeling bloated" literally felt like the death of me. I could not separate my true self from my passing thoughts and feelings. A huge part of my recovery and self-discovery has been my ability to separate my identity from the surface mental sewage that blocks my view of reality.

Through therapy, I realized that I am not my body—I am much more than just my physical form. Kind of weird, but also quite pleasant and freeing. Makes you feel lighter; makes you *live* lighter. I'm not saying that I'm some waif-like spirit, floating on the whimsical current of an indefinable world (that *would* be cool though). What I'm saying is that my physical self—my body, my fleeting feelings and thoughts—do not define *me*.

I am not just me sitting here typing this blog post. I am not me who ate apples with a whole lot of peanut butter for breakfast. I am not me who will take a sip of black iced coffee in about three seconds. I am a conglomeration, a whole melting pot of things and thoughts and feelings and actions and ideas and emotions. I am now and then, and I am more to come. I am so much more than what you see, how I feel right now, and what I think at a given moment.

If you accept and embrace this way of thinking—this "I extend past the fleeting, corporal now"—it makes it so much easier to accept yourself. If you make a mistake, you can just brush it off and move on. You might have *made that mistake,* but that mistake *does not make you.*

I am not dismissing how you feel and what you think in the present moment. Being present and aware of your thoughts and feelings is crucial for happiness as well. But your whole world expands when you stop confining yourself to these drifting, passing mental mutterings. They come and go, and they may help to form who you are, but they are not entirely what you are or all that you have to offer. Not in the least.

So the next time you feel like crap—whether you feel bloated, or embarrassed, or hungover, or ashamed—just remember that what you feel right now is not the whole you. What people see right now is not the whole you. This moment will only define and defeat you if you let it. So don't.

ENJOY THE JOURNEY MORE BY ELIMINATING THE WORD "SHOULD"

by Maelina Frattaroli

> *Tension is who you think you should be. Relaxation is who you are.*

—PROVERB

A friend of mine once said, "If there's a word in the English language I detest, it's 'should.' What a pointless, useless, waste-of-space (euphemism for other choice adjective) word." I think he's right on the money. At the risk of sounding hypocritical, you *should* consider the definition of should, as defined by dictionary.com:

> *Should: must; ought (used to indicate duty, propriety, or expediency): You should not do that.*

There is always something we feel we cannot and *should* not do for fear of humiliation, regret, or having to explain ourselves to others (and sometimes to ourselves). *Should* is an instrument of regret. Maybe one of these sounds familiar to you: I should not have lashed out near the end of my last long-term relationship. He should not have been so insensitive or distant; that way I wouldn't have lashed out. I should really get a grip on life; people must think I'm unmotivated and stagnant. I shouldn't contact him so often; he must think I'm annoying or needy. I should stop acting on my emotions because I'll regret it later. I should clearly try harder because my boss doesn't give me the time of day.

Some of these decisions may not lead to the results you want in life. But does it serve you to tag on a conditional disclaimer to everything you've said or done in the past? It does if you want to, as F. Scott Fitzgerald wrote in *The Great Gatsby,* "beat on, boats against the current, borne back ceaselessly into the past." But in the real, modern world—without prohibition, flappers, speakeasies, jazz, and glam—it doesn't serve you to caveat your life with *should* if you want to experience life, in the moment, at its fullest.

It's not easy to remove this seemingly harmless word from your vocabulary because we're programmed to blame ourselves when things don't go according to plan or as we hoped they would—as if there's something wrong with us. It's almost as though we hold on to *should* to justify who we actually are: human beings with emotions and flaws.

The truth is, we will continue to occasionally make regretful decisions, lash out when we feel emotion, remain stagnant in unfavorable environments for fear of change, send one too many text messages to unresponsive people, or even lie to remove ourselves from uncomfortable situations. All things we're programmed to know we shouldn't do. I say we *should* do all those things (more hypocrisy—just to make a point). We *should* make mistakes sometimes. Why? Simple: so we can learn from them, and, in time, move forward when we know how and why to do things differently. Not just because we should, but because we understand and are equipped to make that change.

I'm on this rocky road to self-discovery in several aspects of my life, and I'm learning to embrace it, even though it's difficult. Right now, my step is to try and distill all the past "should have/could have/what if/if I had/why didn't I say/why didn't he do" lines of thinking, and the illogical "if I had done X, then Y would have happened" mindset.

It's time to throw logic out the window—to analyze life less and live more. I don't know about you, but I'm ready to think for myself, not under the opinions or reign of anyone else. I suspect it won't be easy. I often stumble without being caught; but the next goal is to learn to catch myself. And if occasionally I don't, to remember that wise proverb: *tension is not who I am. It's not who you are, either.*

STOP BEATING YOURSELF UP OVER MISTAKES

by Michelle Ghilotti Mandel

When you lose, don't lose the lesson.

—Unknown

The spiral staircase has always intrigued the yogi designer in me. The visual draw, similarity to DNA, and cosmic patterns, as well as its mathematical genius, could be enough, but the structure can mean even more.

Picture yourself tripping up in work, life, or love. You've made a mistake, said the wrong thing, or didn't come through with your end of the bargain. You think: how did I let that happen? What a fill-in-the-blank I am. I can't believe I did that, *again*. If only I could rewind.

These aren't the greatest feelings—it's true. However, we live our lives in irony. Though we dislike how we feel having just tripped up, we continue to beat ourselves up for it way after the fact. We cause our own suffering. Furthermore, we seem to forget that when we make mistakes, we grow. An atmosphere of growth is integral to happiness. So, create happiness by seeing mistakes as true growth opportunities.

Although yoga, psychology, and conventional wisdom scream at us to live in the moment, I say we are not *just* the present moment. We are very much our past in the most rich and helpful way. We can use past mistakes to yield a shiny new perspective and, in turn, create a new outcome. If we allow them, our mistakes can fuel our awareness. In helping us decide how to act and react in a fresh and fruitful way, mistakes can actually help bring us closer to happiness and further away from (causing our own) suffering.

Picture a most beautiful spiral staircase in Rome, Paris, London, New York, or Barcelona. Visualize its ample room. Now visualize yourself on this staircase, midway up. You're accomplished. You've come all this way. Look up at where you're going and down at where you've come from. Peek around and up at the spirals above; over and down at the spirals below.

Now comes the part that we don't like that's part of being human. You've suddenly tripped up and missed a step, and you've probably done something similar before. Look down at your feet. Yes, you are here, right now, and it's close to before—but not exactly. You are wiser today than yesterday. Though you might feel bad because you're encountering the same or similar problem, this time it's with a different view and perspective.

Accept where you are. You will immediately suffer less. Remember, this is merely one moment in time. It only defines you and your worth if you choose to make it a defining moment. Look down the middle of the staircase at what you've ascended. Keep hold of this view of yourself and see where you are now in comparison. Yes, this human moment has come to find you again, but you're now higher up and can respond from a different place—literally, figuratively, emotionally, and intellectually. Ask yourself: How can I respond from this higher place instead of causing myself pain?

Welcome to your new spiral staircase–inspired mantra: *I have a view. I hold wisdom. I use both.* Think it. Say it. Act on it. Let it create your new character.

I've used the staircase visual and practiced this mantra for a long time. However, it's newest for one particular aspect of life these last two years. In sports and yoga I have always asked a lot of myself. I've competed with myself and failed to listen to my body. I journeyed close to one year with a sports hernia, then chronic sacroiliac (SI) joint pain/lower back issues, and a tear of my adductor during a restorative yoga pose (of all times). I could go on about my wrists, my left shoulder, my neck, and the running injuries, but I think you get the picture.

I did an A+ job at beating myself up, which only added to the extreme sadness of not being active each time I made myself suffer. But that was then, and this is now. I now have wisdom that has changed the way I treat my body. I have proven that I can be gentle to myself but still strong. Also, I have learned an insane amount about the human body.

Though I still like to push when I know it is healthy to do so, I assess from that higher place. I assess where I've been, where I am, where I really want to go, and how I want to feel.

On that next spiral up I remind myself there's no final or "perfect" destination off the staircase of life. It is merely a journey with many similar situations. However, with growing wisdom and a richer perspective, we are better able to deal, enjoy ourselves, and suffer less. It's freeing to know that we are acting from a more intelligent place today versus yesterday, don't you think?

As I sit here typing while icing tendonitis in both arms, I challenge you to give yourself a break next time. *Woe is not you. Wisdom is.*

You can start changing your perspective by using this visual of a staircase. Make it your new BFF. The next time a familiar situation is frustrating you, think, yes, you're confronting something similar again; but this time it's higher up the staircase. Trust and respond from this place. Ask yourself: how can I react differently this time given the learning from last time?

Next, remember that everything transforms. Connect with the fact that with up comes down, with light comes darkness. With down comes up, with darkness comes light. When you find yourself smack in the middle of a day filled with disequilibrium, remember that your equilibrium must be right around the corner. Trust in the flow of your life and that of the universe.

It will help to develop a growth mindset. Accept the idea of a failure en route to your goals. In essence, plan for some roadblocks, nod when they come (you knew they were coming), and move on as quickly as possible.

Lastly, practice saying, "I'm sorry," especially to those you wouldn't normally say it to. Saying these words filled with meaning forces you to move from your comfort zone and look at things from a different side. Healthy, yes, but more importantly, it also brings you closer to the people who make life worth living.

And if all else fails, do a headstand or downward dog. It's difficult to feel and see things the same way if you're upside down.

Namaste. And remember: when in doubt, take the spiral staircase. It really is the most pleasant route. See you there. I'll be the one repeating this mantra, borrowed from Samuel Beckett: "Ever tried. Ever failed. No matter. Try again. Fail again. Fail better."

Top 4 Tips About Forgiving Yourself

1. **Reframe guilt- and shame-driven thoughts to be more self-compassionate.**

When you start getting hard on yourself, recognize that you have a say in what goes on in your head, and consequently, how you feel. Then consciously choose to replace self-judging thoughts with kinder ones. As soon as you recognize you're going down a self-critical path, visualize a red stop sign in your head and replace that thought with, "I made a poor decision, but I am a good person. I am learning from this mistake, and I'm proud of that."

2. **Realize your mistakes only define you if you let them.**

After a huge mistake, you may suddenly have a limited perception of yourself—as if that one decision negated everything good you've done and everything worthwhile about your character. Of course you'll feel horrible about yourself if you think your worst decisions define you. Step back and give yourself some perspective. Ask yourself, "When I'm ninety and looking back on my life, will this really be my focus?" Odds are, it won't. You'll see yourself and your life as a totality, and your mistakes as part of the fabric of your journey.

3. **Remove the phrase "should have" from your vocabulary.**

What's done is done. You did your best—and even if you didn't, it wasn't because you are a bad person. It's because we all trip up sometimes; it's part of being human. Instead of dwelling on what you *should have* done, focus on what you can do right now. Stay in the realm of what you can control. You can't ever go back and change the past; you can't erase the things that you're not proud of. But you can be proud of how you respond to the consequences of what you've done. Whatever quality you wish you embodied before, choose to embody it now. It's not too late to be who you want to be.

4. **Ask yourself how you can respond more wisely than you have in the past.**

Instead of thinking there's something wrong with you for struggling, consider that mistakes are essential to growth—then use this as an opportunity to show yourself how much you have grown. How can you respond to this mistake more wisely than ones past? What insights can you glean from this mistake that may help you improve going forward? How can you leverage this as a learning experience, essentially making it useful?

CHAPTER 5

When You Focus on Getting Approval: Releasing the Need for Validation

THERE IS NOTHING MORE FUTILE AND MORE EXHAUSTING THAN trying to get everyone to like you. For one thing, it's impossible; but more importantly, it's counterproductive. When you adapt yourself to please the varied people you meet, you inevitably lose track of who you actually are—which means no one gets a chance to know you and form a genuine opinion. Perhaps even worse, you end up feeling disingenuous every time you say something you don't really think, believe, or feel, which inevitably chisels away at your self-respect—even if you believe you're being a "good person" by agreeing, conceding, and censoring yourself.

You might look for approval from other people because you want confirmation that you're good enough. Maybe you don't trust your thoughts and opinions, so you look to others to back your decisions.

Or perhaps it's not just about feeling loved, appreciated, and accepted; it could also be about avoiding the pain of rejection, which stings even more if it confirms your worst fears about yourself. According to German psychoanalyst Karen Horney, the need for approval relates to a fear of helplessness and abandonment. None of us wants to feel excluded, disregarded, or otherwise devalued.

We all look for approval from others in some way or another, whether we consciously recognize it or not. It's how we gauge our performance in life. We look to our bosses to confirm we're doing a good job, our loved ones to ensure we're meeting their needs and expectations, and maybe even strangers to confirm that unbiased outsiders recognize our significance and worth. It's natural to crave some level of external feedback. It only becomes detrimental when we give it so much power that every criticism or negative assessment diminishes our self-esteem.

Unhealthy approval seeking can be a difficult habit to break, especially since it's generally rooted in fear; but it *is* possible to place less weight on other people's perceptions and more weight on our own. With focus and effort, we can learn to value ourselves whether other people validate us or not.

How can we stop fearing abandonment and rejection? How can we stop obsessing about other people's opinions? How can we feel more confident, so we stop trying to manipulate how others see us, and focus instead on being who we want to be? Countless Tiny Buddha contributors have addressed these issues on the site, sharing their experiences and insights. Some of those include . . .

REJECTION CAN REVEAL HOW WE'RE REJECTING OURSELVES

by Erin Lanahan

> *Your task is not to seek love, but merely to seek and find all the barriers within yourself that you have built against it.*
>
> —RUMI

Up to a certain point in my life, I was always seeking approval and validation from everything outside of me. All I ever wanted was to feel loved. I longed for this feeling and wondered how the world could be so cruel as to reject me when I was so loving and available. I have since learned that I was not as available as I thought I was.

It has been my experience that everyone who crosses our path is a mirror. They have come because we have called them into our lives to show us something—to teach us how to be more of who we truly are. Our higher selves crave these experiences and relationships, because ultimately, this journey we call life is all about finding everything we want within us rather than without. It's about waking up.

I have learned this after many years of things not turning out the way I wanted them to, feeling as though I was a victim, and that life was just *not fair*. I felt this way until I finally got it—I finally understood that life is happening *for* us. Yes, for us. When I experience the pain of rejection in the external world, it is only because there are still places within myself where I am rejecting myself. As long as I reject myself, I will regularly attract people and situations that reject me, because we attract the people, places, and things that are energetic matches to ourselves.

If I'm conscious about this, I can use these experiences as opportunities to break down the fear that keeps me from fully giving and receiving my own love and love from other people. I have the choice to sink into my truth and be available to the pain I feel, and then to use it as a tool for healing. By giving it my attention, I can then fully feel it and process it.

When we really feel our feelings and allow ourselves to fully have an experience, then the charge within us dissolves and no longer attracts more of itself into our lives. This can be hard to accept at first, because it is much easier to blame someone else for our pain and sorrow. But that is an illusion too. In the end, it is much easier and way more productive to take full responsibility for everything that "happens to us."

If we can live life consciously and authentically, understanding that things do not happen *to* us, but rather *for* us, we can use everything that comes into our lives as experience to our benefit. We can locate all the barriers that keep us from beauty, love, abundance, intimacy, and joy.

Recently, I confessed my feelings of affection to someone who didn't feel the same way for me. I've avoided this for a long time. I was so afraid of feeling rejected that I had pushed my feelings down for almost two years. However, as I grew and evolved, I considered that the entire relationship was there for me to heal. I was meant to look my fear of rejection in the eyes and learn to love myself through it.

So that is exactly what I did. I came clean. I had external integrity and shared my heart with him in a way I never could have imagined doing just a few short months ago. Now that he knows how deeply I care for him, I feel like my wounds are on the mend. I continue to have internal integrity and allow myself to feel all the fears his rejection triggered, such as "I'll never be good enough," or "I'll never be chosen," or "I'll never get what I want because there is something wrong with me."

Previously, I was holding myself back in my interactions with him because I was afraid to feel these things. Once I accepted that this relationship was happening *for* me, I realized I had to risk potential rejection. If I didn't because I didn't feel worthy, my fears would prevent me from attracting the level of intimacy that blossoms in open, honest, loving relationships.

Rejection was the only way through these walls I'd built. It was time to feel the fear and do it anyway, for my own good. Now I'm not afraid of rejection because *I'm* not rejecting me. I can feel gratitude for it, and every other emotion I experience, because all of it is relevant—all of it is there for me to heal my wounds so I can be free. I'm learning to love myself more as I use my life to break down the barriers within me that keep me from returning to love.

Next time you feel unappreciated, frustrated, or rejected, do yourself a favor and use them as opportunities. Put these feelings in your box of healing tools. Then ask yourself: how could these people, places, or things show you the barriers within yourself that keep you from experiencing all the love, peace, and joy you long for? Remember—our external world is a reflection of our internal world. What does your internal world look like? To change within is to change without.

LETTING GO OF INSECURITIES WITH TWO REALIZATIONS

by Emma Brooke

> *What I am is good enough if I would only be it openly.*
> —CARL ROGERS

I used to spend an awful lot of time worrying about people liking me. Or what people thought of me. Or what they thought of the clothes I was wearing. Or whatever. It's taken me a long time to realize two things: most people aren't even taking notice of you (they're too busy worrying about what other people think of them); and of the few who *are* noticing you, the ones who are judging harshly are not the people you want to be around anyway.

Makes sense, right?

It's actually something I'd heard a hundred times before, but it never really sunk in. What made it so hard to believe this is actually the case, and that I should give up caring what people think once and for all? I think, in simple terms, it's built into our human nature. We're social creatures, therefore we want to be sociable; and we think that in order to be sociable, everyone has to like us. Otherwise we would become . . . *gasp!* . . . social outcasts.

Lately, I've been challenging this fear. I recently moved from my small town to London. Capital city, UK. The big smoke (for the United Kingdom). I decided, in my quest to try new things and get healthier, to join the gym at the end of my road. Unfortunately, I've never felt quite at home in a gym. For me, it's almost like that scene in *Pretty Woman* when Julia Roberts walks in to the designer clothing boutique for the first time and all the shop assistants look down their noses at her.

I have to admit, that hasn't actually ever happened at my gym—at all. But it's happening in my head, because in my head I also hear, "You're not as good as them," "They'll think you're stupid," and "You don't fit in here." You've probably had a similar experience at some point in your life. Maybe you were just starting a new job, or meeting your partner's parents for the first time, or walking into your first day of school. The problem is, it's not other people with the problem. It's us.

When I think about everything I assume everyone else is thinking, I see side-glances and sniggers where none really exist. The gym, for me, becomes hard work, not because of the people who go to my gym, but because of how I perceive them to be.

I am currently working on developing a positive attitude. It underlies my whole philosophy on life: Your thoughts create your reality. My natural disposition was always a bit negative. I suspect I developed that attitude partially because my parents taught me that it was important to consider all the options and to be "realistic." That, in itself, is not a bad thing, but I ended up focusing on the negative side of things instead of realizing I had a choice to perceive things differently.

After my experience with the gym, I decided to turn my negative thoughts about other people into positive ones. Instead of dwelling on all the bad things I thought people were thinking, I told myself, "I belong here," "I'm happy here," and "Everyone here likes me."

Everything started to change. I suddenly realized that no one was looking at me strangely. No one cared what I was doing or whether I was as gorgeous as them. (There are super attractive people at my gym!) They were quite happy minding their own business, doing their own thing, and working on themselves—and suddenly I was able to do the same.

We *are* sociable animals, and we want that approval from other people, which for generations has meant conforming to the social norms of our society. But we live in a time when people are far more tolerant of individual differences than ever before. If we can start to accept and be who we are, we just may realize that not only is it okay, but most other people think it's okay, too.

We really can be ourselves if we can remember that it's our perception that matters—and it's a waste of energy to try to see ourselves through other people's eyes. Odds are, they're paying far less attention to us than we think.

YOU ARE GOOD ENOUGH WHETHER OTHER PEOPLE VALIDATE YOU OR NOT

by Alesha Chilton

What other people think of me is none of my business.
—WAYNE DYER

When I was younger I was afraid of being myself. I constantly wanted to conform to others in order to be liked and appreciated. I just wanted to be liked for myself, but I wasn't letting people see that person. I've learned that if you show the real you, not everyone will like you, and that's okay. The people who are worth your time will appreciate you for who you are. And you will have deeper, more meaningful relationships as a result.

I was afraid to think for myself. I was not confident in my decisions, and I let others decide what I should be doing according to their beliefs. I felt like a toy boat being tossed about in the ocean, and it was exhausting.

We don't learn in school what healthy relationships look like and what is and isn't acceptable. We make excuses for other people's behavior, even though it is hurtful to us. We hope that they will change and think that perhaps we can mold them into better people.

In my first relationship, I changed myself completely for the guy. I desperately wanted someone to love me, so I went from being a suburban girl to a country girl—complete with the cowboy boots and belt buckle. But inside I felt empty because I was playing a role. Deep down, I was afraid of being rejected. I didn't think I was worthy of being loved just as I was.

After that, I got into an abusive relationship. I reasoned that he would change into the person he used to be—that maybe I could help him be a better person. Nothing changed. Things just got worse. I let him have control over me, and ultimately I became depressed and fearful. Love isn't supposed to be fearful. Love means accepting a person, flaws and all. But it's also about mutual respect for each other. It's about fully appreciating a person without trying to change them. It's about free will.

I got pregnant in college, and I lost a whole group of friends who judged me for it. But looking back, I realize this experience weeded out friends who weren't truly there for me. My true friends, on the other hand, threw a surprise baby shower for me and loved me unconditionally. This is what people do when they see and accept you for who you are. This is what we open up to when we do the same for ourselves.

I finished college with help from my parents and am now earning my master's degree. Many people asked if I was quitting college. They doubted that I could be a student and a mother. But I had faith in myself. For the first time, I felt confident, whether everyone liked me or not.

As I grew into a stronger woman, I realized that who I am is wonderful, and that no one was going to convince me otherwise or try to change me. I also decided to stop hoping I could change other people. I took things one day at a time, because looking at the big picture was too daunting and overwhelming. I knew that one day I would meet someone who loved me for me, and that I would love them for them—when the time was right.

Having a child has helped me appreciate the present moment and beauty around me. My daughter doesn't get stressed out about the past or the future. She doesn't worry about what others think of her. She simply dances around the living room, plays with her toys, and laughs without worries or cares. She appreciates flowers and sunlight. Seeing her live reminds me of who and how I want to be.

The present moment is all we have, and we deserve to enjoy it. Worrying is exhausting. It drains you mentally and physically. And in the end, nothing gets accomplished except worry itself. So why do we do it? Because we mistake worrying for taking positive action. We feel as if fretting over an outcome can change the situation, when in reality it cannot.

One time while I was pregnant I was at the grocery store and I thought this old woman was giving me dirty looks. She was glaring at my empty ring finger. I felt certain I knew what she was thinking: "Look at that unmarried pregnant woman. She's such a sinner and a drain on society." I ended up getting nervous and hurried to leave. Upon going out the door, I realized that I had left my milk in the store.

At that point I realized how ridiculous it was. So what if she *was* judging me? Why should I let someone else get me that frazzled? I realize now that I can only open up to all the good I deserve in life if I stop obsessing about what people think of me and fully realize that, just as I am, I am good enough.

We are all good enough, and we all deserve the best. We just have to believe it.

LET GO OF THE NEED FOR APPROVAL

by Sacha Crouch

> *Criticism is something you can easily avoid by saying nothing, doing nothing, being nothing.*
>
> —ARISTOTLE

The need for approval kills freedom. Trust me, I know, because I spent my entire life seeking approval until I realized it was a waste of time and didn't work anyway. My desire to get people to like me was the motivation behind the majority of my choices and actions in my early life. Queen of the social chameleons, I mastered the art of telling people what they wanted to hear and being someone they would find impressive—all the while worrying incessantly about what others thought of me, fearing criticism, and holding myself back as a result.

When I first started building my coaching business, this craving for acceptance caused me to hide from opportunities where the potential for reward was high, but the possibility for criticism was equally as large. As an example, one of my first client referrals was to coach the CEO of a major corporation. It's painful to admit that I told my client I wasn't the right person for the job and referred them to someone else.

My need for approval created immense anxiety about the value I provided for my clients and caused me to spend far too much time on tasks in order to perfect them. It got to the point where I was wasting so much time and losing so many opportunities that I had to make a big decision: either let the business go or learn how to get over myself! Fortunately, I chose the latter. I created a plan to learn to let go of needing others' approval (well, at least letting go enough that it would no longer sabotage my success). Here I am, seven years later, running the same business with much greater ease and success as a result.

Can you relate to these issues? Do you constantly make choices to avoid disapproval or criticism, rather than choosing to pursue what is most valuable, effective, or important to you? Do you hold yourself back from speaking your opinions or hide your true self? This is something you can, and, dare I say, *must* change if you want to be happy in your life and successful in your career. It *is* possible to change.

I have identified four levels of approval-seeking behavior:

The need for approval—low performance. Your need for approval negatively impacts your performance—you avoid doing important things, feel anxiety and fear, and get stuck in worry and rumination. Wanting people to like you results in declining new opportunities, being too nervous to perform effectively, and showing signs of avoidance, such as apathy, withdrawal, analysis paralysis, and giving up. If this rings true for you, recognize how the need for approval is holding you back from doing the important things. When you feel those familiar constricting feelings, remind yourself of everything you stand to gain by doing your best, whether other people validate you or not—all the opportunities, possibilities, and positive feelings you could enjoy if only you made an effort. Once you shift your focus from what you might not receive from others to what you can provide for yourself, you will be free to achieve and create what you want in life with much less stress and effort, because you are currently exhausting yourself through avoidance.

The need for approval—high performance. Although you're a high achiever and get great results in your life, it is often at the expense of everything else. The need for approval in this case results in doing too much, feeling anxiety, worrying, being unable to stop ruminating about challenges, trying to please everyone, not making time for yourself, working too hard, and being unable to say no. If this is you, focus on how the need for approval is causing you to do too much instead of only what is important, and to do things for others at the expense of yourself.

Self-acceptance—low performance. In this instance, what others think of you has little impact on your decision-making about how to spend your time. However, your performance is low due to other motivational factors, such as being unaware of what is important to you, what drives you, and what makes you happy. Hence, you may be stuck doing work you don't really enjoy and have habits that hinder your performance, or alternatively, you may not have the skills to work effectively at what you are doing. If this is you, focus your energy on getting in touch with what really matters to you. Start to listen to what you really want in your life and act on this to make it happen. Life becomes much more effortless when you are living in alignment with what is important to you.

Self-acceptance—high performance. This is a place where you make decisions based on what is right for you. You make effective choices with your time, are okay with saying no when it is required, and are committed to only doing that which is important and valuable to you. In this space, you spend less time in your head worrying about people and situations and more time just getting things done. You don't need to be busy in order to appear successful. Instead, you choose to measure success by doing what matters to you and charting your results. This is a collaborative space where you lead and connect effectively with others without being at their beck and call.

Once you've identified where you are, it's time to do something about it! Below are a handful of strategies to help you get to fourth stage, high-performing self-acceptance.

The first step is to strengthen your core foundation so that you will no longer feel the need to look to others to feel good about your choices and decisions. Keep a self-appreciation journal, where you start acknowledging daily or a few times a week the things you're most proud of about yourself: choices you've made, insights you've learned, things you like about yourself, times you've stayed true to yourself, or whatever feels right for you.

Second, practice letting go of seeking validation for your choices about who you choose to be. This means noticing your language, self-talk, and behavior, and identifying when it is coming from wanting someone else to say you're okay, that you've made the right choice, or that you've done the right thing. Instead, when you do make a decision, check in with yourself that it feels right, remind yourself that it is your choice, and that you've considered your options carefully, and give yourself validation for just being you.

Last, be honest with yourself when you take on a new task or commitment. Sit down and evaluate your weekly tasks and ask yourself what is really necessary and important, and what you're doing to please others. Then slowly work through the "people-pleasing" list and eliminate those tasks.

The need for approval doesn't have to control your life—not if you choose to move past it.

Top 4 Tips About Releasing the Need for Approval

1. **When you deal with rejection, recognize in what ways you're rejecting yourself.**

   No one likes rejection, but it's infinitely more painful when we see it through the lens of our own self-rejection. We magnify what we think we see when it seems to confirm our worst fears about ourselves. When you feel someone's rejecting you, step back and ask yourself: how could my interpretation of this be a mirror for what's going on within me? What can this teach me about how I reject myself, and how I can change that?

2. **Challenge your assumption that other people are judging you.**

   When we worry about what other people think, we often assume they're judging us harshly. Recognize that they're likely not thinking about you nearly as much as you think; and that, just like you, they're struggling with their own insecurities. When you stop focusing on the negative things you assume other people are thinking, you're free to focus on your own thoughts—and to change them to be more positive and empowering.

3. See it as a positive sign if some people don't like you.

If you're being yourself without censoring yourself to please your audience, it's inevitable that some people will dislike you. While this may be uncomfortable, it's the only way to open yourself up to people who will appreciate and value you for who you really are. Whenever someone seems to reject you, instead of thinking there's something lacking in you, see this as a sign that this person is not a good match for a meaningful relationship. Then affirm to yourself that you're creating the possibility of meeting other people who are.

4. Keep a self-appreciation journal.

Keep a log of all the things you appreciate about yourself: the compassion you show other people, the choices you've made to honor your instincts, the times when you've bounced back from difficult situations. When you feel like you need someone else to validate you, turn to this list and use it as a way to validate yourself. Let this be a reminder that you're a strong, capable person—someone who can make decisions without needing other people to agree with them.

CHAPTER 6

When You Think Other People Are Better: Letting Go of Comparisons

It all starts so innocently: We see someone else who seems to have something we want, and we start assessing how we measure up. At first we might convince ourselves we're doing something positive—using them for motivation—and perhaps we are. But oftentimes we're not merely recognizing their choices and accomplishments and then allowing them to inspire our own. We're also thinking about everything we've failed to do and judging ourselves for not stacking up.

We're collecting evidence that other people are better than us, and in the process decreasing our odds of growing and improving, since self-judgment can often feel crippling. Instead of recognizing that we hold the same light and value, regardless of how things look externally, we start looking for proof that we don't. We see all the goals we haven't reached. All the relationships we haven't fostered. And all the expectations we haven't met. Then we question *why* we seem to have failed in so many ways. What do other people have that we don't?

Stuck as we get in our negative self-assessments, we may decide to swing the pendulum the other way and compare ourselves to those less fortunate. Surely we should feel grateful that we have homes, jobs, and stability, unlike many others who aren't as well off. But this is still a choice to see ourselves in relation to everyone else, as if we need to know we're not the lowest in the pecking order in order to avoid feeling low. If we should go through a tough time and lose those things we told ourselves to appreciate, we may feel completely unhinged, as if we have no sense of value because we have less than almost everyone else.

To some extent, it's natural to compare ourselves to others; we learn from a young age to gauge our progress by seeing what our peers are doing. But we set ourselves up for dissatisfaction and even depression if we let our comparisons convince us we're intrinsically inferior—and then let a sense of helpless negativity convince us that this will never change. It might take effort, but we have the power to see ourselves with an objective appreciation for who we are as individuals, regardless of our accomplishments. We have the ability to recognize other people's successes and strengths without criticizing ourselves in response. And we have the capacity to foster our own strengths so we can create lives that feel satisfying, whether other people seem to have more or not.

Countless Tiny Buddha contributors have addressed these issues on the site, sharing their experiences and insights. Some of those include . . .

STOP MAKING COMPARISONS AND START VALUING YOURSELF

by Margie Beiswanger

It takes courage to grow up and become who you really are.

—E. E. CUMMINGS

It seems like everywhere I look, I don't measure up.

I was giving a presentation recently and noticed that several people seemed bored or distracted. I looked around the room to gauge my audience's response to something I said and found myself thinking, "Am I good enough? Am I providing what this group needs?" Suddenly, I felt sure that another more talented presenter would have done a better job.

Later, my friend and I were casually flipping through old photos, and we both lamented that we were younger and thinner in them. We chuckled and then sighed. I commented that I didn't like how I looked in the photos, and she said that I looked great. I started to dispute her out of habit. I thought I should look better somehow. Do you know that feeling? It seems as if I can't be satisfied with how I look because I should be something more.

There are people all around me who are more talented, thinner, wealthier, happier, nicer, and luckier. You name it and there is someone who's got more of it or is better at it than me. Ever feel that way?

And yet, our tendency is to continue to compare ourselves with others—over and over again. Demoralizing and useless as it is, we keep doing it. We're pretty much on autopilot at this point. Why oh why do we engage in such a fruitless mental activity? Do we think it's going to make us feel better in some miraculous way? Do we think it's going to motivate us to excel?

What's that mental comparison thing you do ever done for you? Does it really motivate you to get going on your diet and exercise plan or your savings plan or your new career path? I didn't think so. I know it doesn't work that way for me.

I say, "Enough!" Let's stop mentally assessing our worth by comparing it to others. Think about it. What does your status, your value, your worth have to do with anyone else's? Really think about that.

In reality, what does my weight have to do with anyone else's? How is my net worth any different—in value—if I say it should be equal to or greater than someone else's? It's just not. Doing the mental comparison thing doesn't change a thing about me in reality. I am what I am. Right now. And that's the reality. I choose to value myself, just as I am.

I am a unique individual. So are you. We all are. The next time you find that you're comparing yourself with someone else, remind yourself that "I am me and I'm proud of that." You've got to let that sink in. You are your own person. There's no one quite like you. Comparisons are irrelevant! How freeing is that? Add that to your mental repertoire: "I'm unique, so comparisons are irrelevant."

When we're doing the mental comparison thing, we're focusing on what others have that we think we don't. Find something that you do have—a trait, a possession, a relationship, a value—that you can feel good about. This has nothing to do with the other person. This is about not comparing, so there's no need to try to one up them in your mind.

For example, the next time I wish I had a big vacation house on the shore, I can remember: I may not have a vacation house, but I do have a loving family to share my time with. If I find myself comparing my body to another person's (perhaps a celebrity or someone younger than me), I can flip my focus and remind myself of how well my body has served me all these years. I can remind myself of other positive traits—that I'm a generous friend, a loving partner, a talented cook, and a funny person.

Flip your focus and remind yourself of all that you are instead of focusing on what you think you aren't.

Let's move away from devaluing ourselves and others. Let's be good enough, just as we are, and celebrate that. Instead of always finding ways that we don't measure up, let's celebrate the things about ourselves and others that make us unique, that make us who we are. Let's celebrate the fact that we're all different, and we all have something to contribute to this big, beautiful world, just as we are today.

What is one small thing you can do today to embrace your individuality and celebrate yourself, just as you are?

LET GO OF FEAR BY STOPPING THE STORIES IN YOUR HEAD

by Angela Gunn

> *The greater part of human pain is unnecessary. It is self-created as long as the unobserved mind runs your life.*
>
> —ECKHART TOLLE

For a very long time fear has controlled me. It has paralyzed me, kept me living in desperate situations, and stopped me from living the life of my dreams. It has only been with age and the practice of mindfulness these last few years that I have finally come to recognize the fear within me and begun the process of facing it.

By facing fear, I don't mean that I've started BASE jumping, purposely trapped myself in elevators, or allowed tarantulas to climb all over my body. I mean that I've sat in meditation, watched the fears arise, and rather than react to them or allow them to become part of the stories that make up my life, I've observed them in my mind from a distance. I've felt how fearful thoughts manifest in my body, and I've moved into that physical discomfort in order to pay attention to fear in a way I've never allowed myself to do before.

When I think about the compulsive and addictive activities that have kept me stuck in a place of fear in the past, they all come from stories that play through my head every day. For example, I shop to feel better about myself. I believe that the pair of celebrity-endorsed high heels I've just bought will make me glamorous enough to fit in with the goddesses I see around me, and, therefore, help me feel accepted. Interestingly, I don't feel bad about myself unless I'm comparing myself with others. Therefore, in the comparing, I'm looking at others who have what I don't and fearing that I'm unstylish or not beautiful enough.

When the new pair of high heels I've been wearing to work every day go unnoticed, start to slowly destroy my feet, and still haven't prompted an invite to the "right" parties, I give up and start to search the fridge. I discover a tub of ice cream or a pack of cookies that may not make me more beautiful or accepted, but they help fill my stomach up and create a fullness in the exact place that fear is beginning to dig a deeper and deeper hole inside of me.

When that sick feeling starts rising again, this time from the mix of cookies and cream atop a base of fear, I sit in the comfiest chair I can find and reach for the remote control. Rather than listen to the personal derision on repeat in my mind, I watch reruns of my favorite reality show. I can then cheer the reality star on as I would a friend. Or, I can sit and degrade them to make myself feel better by deflecting the meanest thoughts I have going through my head from myself onto them.

I would love to say that after this fear-based pity and hatred party I would choose to hit the shore with my trusty longboard to work off that ice cream, but unless that board comes with a QWERTY keyboard, I'm more inclined to stay at home. Only after watching other people live their busy lives does it actually register that I should reach out and connect with my friends.

After having destroyed my feet in high heels, eaten an entire quart of ice cream all by myself, and vegged out in front of the TV in my PJs, I hardly feel like getting dolled up to go out for some face-to-face time. Therefore, the next best source of connection is my new best friend—the Internet. After returning a few pokes, commenting on a couple friends' pictures, and then checking my homepage incessantly to see if anyone online has responded to my posts, the night drags on. I continually stare at the glowing screen as the minutes tick by, unable to disconnect myself from the cyber world and face the fear of being alone with my self-pity and self-hatred.

Can you believe that this entire fear-based cycle of self-pity and hatred grew from a simple comparison of what I was wearing to those around me? Unbelievable, right? Not really. Having observed my mind, I've come to understand that a good amount of my suffering starts by making comparisons and then creating stories in my head.

Encouragingly, I am not alone in this. However, it is unfortunate to realize that many people who suffer in the same way I do will never learn how to curb their own suffering. They will never give themselves the time to sit, reflect, and watch what comes up in their minds without becoming involved in the stories.

If you would like to take more control over your mind and your suffering, the best practices I know are meditation and mindfulness. To become more mindful, recognize first that you are solely responsible for the thoughts your mind produces. While you can't stop your mind completely, you can take control over it and create moments of peace for yourself.

When thoughts or fear arise, try to do the following as soon as you are aware of what's taking place in your mind and body: Stop. Take a long, deep breath in and out. In your mind say "in" as you breathe in and "out" as you breathe out in order to ground yourself in the present moment. Then, feel the ground beneath your feet. Notice the way your clothes feel against your skin, the wind against your face, the sun on your cheeks. Listen to the birds singing, the rain falling around you, or the ticking of a nearby clock. All this will ground you in the present moment. Even if thoughts want to drag you away with them, coming back to recognize the breath will give you the control you need to prevent this from happening.

Follow these steps until you feel that the thought or storyline in your mind has moved on, or until you feel that the pull of your thought or fear has dissipated slightly. At this point you can return to whatever you were doing, and hopefully you will have prevented yourself from suffering in that moment.

Unfortunately, these steps are by no means a quick fix in saving you from the suffering we all encounter every day. In fact, at first it will take all your energy and resolve to not react to what your mind and ego are doing. It's also quite possible that even after you've covered these steps you will still get lost in your thoughts and fears by comparing yourself to others.

Whether you compare yourself to others or not isn't the point. The point is that you've finally managed to sit down and look at your thoughts and fear. Once you have done this, you've begun the process of taking back control of your mind and your life.

No doubt, occasionally you'll also stop and find yourself right in the middle of buying something you don't really need or switching on the TV without thinking about what you're doing. As long as you notice when you're midway through handing your credit card to the lovely salesperson, you're on your way to conquering your mind.

The more you practice mindfulness, the better you will get at it. The key to all this is not giving up. I'm not saying you'll be able to climb to the top of the Burj Al Khalifa on your next trip to Dubai or take a shower with eight beady spider eyes hanging out on the showerhead above you. But you will be able to stop the stories in your head instead of feeling a pull to distract yourself from all the pain they cause you.

So why not give it a shot. Can it really hurt? Well it might, but it'll hurt for all the right reasons.

RELEASE JEALOUSY AND CELEBRATE YOUR GREATNESS

by Kayla Albert

> *Why compare yourself with others? No one in the entire world can do a better job of being you than you.*
>
> —UNKNOWN

When I arrived home after a brief stint living in another state, I was anxious to reconnect with places from my childhood and the friends I'd left behind. However, while I was healing from a heart-wrenching break up, suffering through sleepless nights on my parents' rock-hard couch, and mulling over where all my freelance writing work had gone, my friends seemed to be successful, happy, and right on track.

Realizing that I had hit rock bottom and that it had crippled my self-esteem, my friends gathered around me, taking shifts to ensure that I wouldn't drown in my overwhelming grief. Yet, while their love and support was what got me through, seeing each of their lives so clearly flourishing added another emotion to my already full load: jealousy. Jealousy is a sneaky bugger—a pot-stirrer that likes to aid the ego in pointing out flaws you'd rather just sweep under the rug. It serves as a reminder of all the success you don't have, the experiences you haven't had, the relationships you'd like to have—basically everything that makes you feel "less than."

I spent the next few months wallowing in comparisons, staring longingly at couples clutching hands as they walked down the street, watching people hustle to their well-paying jobs, and picturing myself in the beautiful homes that others had the ability to purchase. While I knew with every cell in my body that I wanted to be somewhere different, doing something different, jealously kept me rooted firmly in place—a place plagued by lack and thoughts of "if only."

Once I realized that the circumstances wouldn't change until I did, I noticed that entertaining this toxic emotion was getting me nowhere but deeper in my hole of self-pity. That was when jealousy and I parted ways, leading me to some very powerful realizations.

First, I realized that being anything less than happy for others was blocking my own chance at happiness and success. Like attracts like, so by ruminating in the idea that you don't have what someone else has, you're simply attracting more of what you're feeling: lack. This means you are actually pushing away the very things you're craving. Yet, if you are able to celebrate in the successes of others, you are sending a very clear message to the universe: "I'll have some of that too, please!"

It all comes down to the energy of the emotions you're carrying. Frowning on another person's good fortune doesn't feel good; therefore, it can't be creating good things. Feeling excited for someone feels good; therefore, it can help create more good things, for you and for them.

Second, seeing the positive experiences other people were having opened me up to possibilities. When someone else lands a killer job with an impressive paycheck, it gives you something to shoot for. It can show you the amazing possibilities that are already present in the world. This also allows us to confront one negative belief we carry with us as a society: there isn't enough to go around. So, if one person gets something we want, the chances of us getting the same thing are significantly diminished. The truth is, there are more opportunities out there than we think. We simply have to work for them.

Finally, I realized that everything is temporary, and the tables are constantly turning. Realizing that things are always changing can do wonders in all areas of your life—especially when it comes to dealing with jealousy. The monetary wealth you see a friend experiencing could be gone within a year. The relationship you witness and long for could be over within a month. The string of unfortunate circumstances you've been struggling with could turn around in a day. I'm not implying we should take solace in knowing that other people's blessings are temporary, but rather that it helps to realize *everything* in life is, for all of us. We are not the only people who go through hard times. Circumstances are constantly changing, so to spend a great deal of time and energy fretting over them or wishing for something different is, frankly, a waste.

Appreciating *what is* makes "what could be" even sweeter. If you're able to express gratitude for the experience you are having right now—no matter how negative it may look on the surface—you'll have a greater capacity for appreciating the positive experiences when they begin to show up. Maybe you don't have the career success or relationship satisfaction of those around you, but by working through anything that is less than ideal, you are achieving something great: growth. And growth will make room for the changes you've been waiting for.

Jealousy planted one glaring misconception in my mind: who I was simply wasn't enough. I have since realized that the hardships I was experiencing weren't meant to point out my inadequacies, but to create an entirely new life experience that was more fulfilling and more . . . me.

What jealousies do *you* need to kick to the curb?

WHY THE GRASS IS NEVER GREENER AND HOW TO BE HAPPIER TODAY

by Katy Cowan

> *If you worry about what might be, and wonder what might have been, you will ignore what is.*
>
> —UNKNOWN

Lifestyle. Opportunities. Wealth. Just think how far we've come in the past hundred years—especially when you look at what we have today compared with our great grandmothers' generation. My great grandmother married very young, lived in the same place her whole life, and had eleven children. She never had a career and never got a chance to go on a vacation. Her life was hard, poor, and lacking in any real opportunity.

I wonder if she ever dreamed about moving to another city, or transforming her life, or seeing the world with just a backpack. I bet she did, but back then there weren't as many opportunities as we have today. Thanks to technology, the Internet, and an improved society, our lifestyles are completely transformed. We have choices. We can live pretty much anywhere we want. We can travel and see the world. We can secure jobs on the other side of the planet. We can start our own businesses and serve clients thousands of miles away. It's definitely an exciting time.

When there is a wealth of opportunities, choices, and places we could choose to live, you'd think we'd all be happy, right? Wrong. You see, the problem with having choices is that we become restless. We can't settle on what we already have or be satisfied with what we've got, because we'll always be wondering about the next big thing. It's called the "grass is always greener" syndrome. We think someone else is having a better time elsewhere. We make ourselves miserable by constantly thinking about the unknown in an endless quest to find happiness.

We lie awake at night torturing ourselves over what we should do next, wondering if we're missing out on something big. We feel we're wasting our lives if we're not doing something more important. There's also this sense of time pressure, particularly with my generation, who had the saying, "The world is your oyster" drilled into us from a young age. This means there can be a sense of urgency, because we feel like we're running out of time and should be doing something greater or somehow we'll fail.

We also want to think that we're special and that our lives are destined to be adventurous, thrilling, and hugely successful. And when they're not turning out that way? We become depressed. We want more. And we spend all of our time and energy on focusing on what we don't have rather than counting our blessings.

Some of us might start to move around a lot—often to find the "perfect" city or town, somewhere we can call "home," somewhere we'll be happy. Others might jump from one job or relationship to the next, never fully committing to anything. But once we've made that leap to the other side—once we've moved to where we thought the grass would be greener and where we'd be happy—we discover that it is no different. We start to wonder about the grass being greener elsewhere. We are never truly happy when we have "grass is greener" syndrome.

Focusing on things we don't have is a recipe for disaster. It only leads to a miserable existence and causes us to forget what's most important—and that's what's happening right now. As John Lennon once said, "Life is what happens to you while you're busy making other plans." And that's certainly true.

We all seem to be victims of ignoring what's actually happening right at this very moment, which is only natural when we have so many choices and opportunities available to us. We can forget the whole point of happiness, and that's peace of mind, acceptance, and mindfulness. Essentially, it's being happy no matter where you are in the world, or what you're doing, or whom you're with.

Being mindful quiets the mind and brings us a sense of peace that no other quest for a "perfect life" could ever bring. Mindfulness helps you to appreciate life as it happens. It stops us from agonizing over what might've been or what could be. It just brings us back to the present.

Don't get me wrong—opportunity is a marvelous thing, and I only wish my great grandmother had the choices I enjoy today. But I'm slowly coming to realize that my great grandmother might've been just fine with her lifestyle. She was quite possibly happier than me. Her life was simple, and perhaps there's a clue in that. Maybe the simple life is where we can all find peace.

Yes—embrace everything that comes along. Yes—go out and see the world and enjoy everything this life has to offer. But whenever you feel yourself losing focus and wondering about where you'll be happy next, bring yourself back to the present, look at what you already have, look around you, and enjoy the moments that are happening right now. Find peace in reading a good book, doing some gardening, going for a walk in the countryside. Take in the sights, smells, and sounds, and breathe deeply. Start to notice what is happening right now, and I guarantee you'll find peace.

Because happiness isn't about where you live or the things you do. It isn't about being on an impossible mission to do everything, see everywhere, and accomplish everything you've ever dreamed. Happiness is a state of mind. How you achieve it is by building a life around your current location. Making new friends, settling into a routine, finding ways in which to enjoy "the moment" rather than dwelling on all the things you could be doing or the places you could be visiting.

Remember that all we ever have is right now. Forget about the past. Don't worry about the future. Take each day as it comes. And most of all, stop thinking that the grass is greener, because it never really is.

Top 4 Tips About Releasing Comparisons

1. **Flip your focus from what you *aren't* to what you *are*.**

   Focusing on what others seem to have that you think you lack makes you feel less-than. Instead of making comparisons identifying other people as better, reinforce something about yourself that you feel is valuable. For example, if you catch yourself thinking, "He's more successful in his career," remind yourself, "I'm proud that I do something that makes a difference in the world and operate with integrity." Keep the focus on what you're doing right, not on what you assume you're doing wrong.

2. **Stop the fearful mental stories that lead you into self-destructive territory.**

   If you start comparing yourself to others and then shutting down in response to this story, see the story as separate from you—not a truth you need to escape, but an illusion you can release. Instead of responding to the story with compulsive behaviors, see it as a prison that you can escape by letting go. It might help to write them down and burn the paper. Breathe deeply and ground yourself in your body by recognizing the sights, sounds, and smells around you. Then ask yourself, "What would I want to do with this moment if I weren't reacting to my fear of inadequacy?"

3. Get excited about what you can do instead of discouraged by what you think you can't.

See someone doing something that inspires you? If it's genuinely something you want—a possibility that gets you excited, and not just something you think you *should* do—see this as an opportunity to redefine your goals and dreams. Then focus on what you can do to start living in that possibility today. It's not about getting somewhere in the future; it's about doing something right now that makes you feel passionate, proud, and fulfilled. What tiny action can you take today to be the person you want to be?

4. Focus on what you can enjoy right now.

Regardless of what else you could be doing and how other people seem to be excelling, you have countless opportunities to enjoy this day. And really, this is what you want—not what other people seem to do or have, but the positive feelings you assume they feel in response. Make it a priority to create those positive feelings for yourself by engaging with the world, connecting with good friends, or appreciating your surroundings. You're more likely to feel good about yourself when you stop pressuring yourself to do and become more and simply let yourself be.

CHAPTER 7

When You're Trying to Fill a Void: Learning to Complete Yourself

IT'S A COMFORTING ILLUSION, THAT EVERYTHING WILL MAKE SENSE and feel better when we find someone else to share our lives with. If there's one thing we all want, it's enduring happiness, and we learn from a young age that happily ever after is a two-person proposition. So we can easily end up waiting, not with a healthy resolve, for something that feels right, but with a sense that life is somehow lacking until we're able to find it. We end up looking toward *someday*, hoping, wishing, and willing the future to include someone who might complete us.

We may even convince ourselves there's something wrong with us if we're unattached, and start pressuring ourselves to somehow change or improve to better attract our soul mate—as if there's one person out there we're each meant to be with, and we're running out of time to find them. Armed with all this stress, fear, and need, it can be temping to get into a relationship that, deep down, we know isn't right. It's even easier to stay there, afraid of walking away and never finding something better.

It's natural and instinctive to want connection and intimacy; but it's an entirely different thing to believe we need those things right now in order to feel whole and happy. In fact, we're likely to feel disappointed when we find them if we placed unrealistic expectations on how they'd change our feelings and our lives. It's an ironic thing, searching for love. We often seek it outside ourselves because we feel so unworthy, yet it's that same belief that makes it hard to trust it when we finally find it. We want validation to feel we're enough, but we're never really able to feel worthy if we don't already believe we are. In other words: we can't ever find in someone else the love and acceptance we aren't willing or able to give ourselves. No person, thing, or experience can fill the void of our self-rejection, and none of it will be satisfying until we believe that, just as we are, we are worthy of enjoying it.

Connection, belonging, security—these are fundamental human needs. How do we enable ourselves to meet them without feeding into the idea that we're somehow lacking? How can we learn to feel whole and complete just as we are, and also open ourselves up to healthy, fulfilling relationships? How can we fill the void we feel so that we can appreciate other people for who they are instead of depending on them to help us do the same for ourselves? Countless Tiny Buddha contributors have addressed these questions on the site, sharing their experiences and insights. Some of those include . . .

LEARNING TO STOP CLINGING TO PEOPLE: KNOW THAT YOU ARE LOVED

by Elizabeth Garbee

> *As long as you make an identity for yourself out of pain, you cannot be free of it.*
>
> —ECKHART TOLLE

I have a heart condition. Not one that you could see on an X-ray, or even one that you would find in a medical textbook. For as long as I can remember, I have felt like my heart had a gaping hole in it—and I've been stuffing anyone and anything into that space to try and feel a little less empty. A little less alone.

The first day of my freshman year in college, I met a girl. We spent the rest of the day together and discovered we had an uncanny amount in common, including our values and a passion for the violin. We even had the same name. So I decided then and there that she would be that college friend everyone talks about, that friend with whom you share everything and never lose touch, even after you're both old and gray.

I decided she was the perfect shape to fill the hole in my heart. I then proceeded to spend as much time as possible with her and her friends, ignoring the people I had grown close to in my dorm. I even declined invitations from classmates to go out to eat, get a coffee, or even just go with them to the library; I wanted to be available in case she and her friends decided they wanted to do something with me. Yet, even though I thought I had finally found a group of people that made me feel complete, there was always this underlying fear—a fear that they were just pretending to like me, that I was a second-class citizen in this clique.

And then she broke the news to me. "You make our group dynamic awkward," she said. "We think you should go find some other friends."

I was devastated. My heart now felt even more empty and alone than it did before I met her, because I had built an identity for myself based on a friendship I had forced—a relationship I had made fit simply because it was there and available. After that, I slowly started spending time with my other friends and started enjoying their company again, but I still withdrew and isolated myself. I couldn't imagine that anyone would want to spend time with me if she and her friends didn't, and that perception made it almost impossible to believe anything good anyone said about me.

A few months later, an old crush came back into my life. We had been talking sporadically for years, but this relationship was also forced. I loved him desperately and had told him so on several occasions; while he didn't feel the same, he still cared enough about me to want to keep in touch. But the more we started talking, the more I became convinced that there was finally something there—and I came to believe that he wanted something more than just friendship.

So, a year later, I had completely invested my self-worth and self-esteem in this guy's occasional emails and even rarer phone calls. Though our conversations were a little awkward and a bit strained, I continued to read between lines that simply weren't there. When I asked him if he wanted to try a "formal relationship," he looked confused and completely blindsided. He said no.

I stopped talking to him and harbored a highly combustible combination of anger and resentment. My carefully constructed identity, made from assumptions and misinterpreted signals, had just come crashing down—and I was left, again, wondering how anyone could love and value me if this man I had known for eight years didn't. At least not the way I wanted him to.

My overwhelming desire to feel loved and wanted by one person in particular had once again blinded me—and this pain I had created for myself, this empty ache in my chest, was the only thing I could feel.

The Buddhists have a word for this: *samskara*. A pattern, a habit you get into that is so seductive you almost want to continue the cycle. In my case, a cycle of self-inflicted suffering and abuse. I was convinced that because I wasn't in a relationship, because I had never had a significant other (I hadn't even been kissed), I wasn't loved. Worse yet, I started to think that I just wasn't the kind of person anyone could come to love in that way.

It didn't matter that I had a good network of friends at school who loved and cared about me; it didn't matter that I had incredibly loving parents and a brother who adored me; it even didn't matter that I couldn't seem to find a single person I had ever met who didn't like me. I had wanted love from a specific kind of person because I was convinced that was the missing piece in my heart. And because I hadn't found it yet, I had measured my life that was full of love and support and still found it wanting.

This guy and I just recently started talking again, and though we've worked through a lot of the pain and confusion in our relationship, my blood pressure still skyrockets when I simply hear his voice. This reaction isn't because of him in particular, but because he serves as a powerful reminder of all the pain I've created for myself over the years by weaving fantasies around the people I choose to cling to.

I see him again in a week. While most people prepare for guests by cleaning the house, stocking the fridge, and making sure the spare bed is turned down, I'm doing something a little different: I'm working on getting to know myself. If I don't remember who I am independent of what he thinks of me, I'll just get sucked back in; and the disappointment that we aren't what we "could have been" will continue to keep me from being the person I have always wanted to be—the person who loves herself for who she is, not for which person chooses to love her.

I'm not going to pretend that this will be easy. Ripping away Band-Aids and actually facing the wound underneath never is. But this time, I know I'm going to be fine. I know this because, even though it may not come from him, or her, or anyone else I've tried to stuff inside my heart, I am surrounded by love—unconditional love that is freely available to anyone who knows to look for it.

No matter where you are in your journey, no matter what you do for a living, or even what you eat for dinner, *you are loved*. And if this samskara has taught me anything, it's that only when you've opened your heart to the love that already surrounds you can you begin to see it elsewhere.

LOVING WITHOUT LOSING YOURSELF

by Jennifer Gargotto

> *We love because it is the only true adventure.*
>
> —Nikki Giovanni

Last night I sat with an old friend who recently broke up with his girlfriend. He's sad. She's sad. I don't think it was time for them to give up yet; he's exhausted and disagrees. He says he thinks that he just loves to love. When you love to love, he says, it's impossible to separate the act of loving from the person you're actually supposed to love. He thinks that he's too much in love with the *idea* of love to actually know what he wants. And so, he argues, giving her another chance would be futile.

I know what he means, because I love to love, too. When I met my boyfriend, Chase, I thought I had been in love before. In fact, I was positive of it. I had built a life out of a dating and relationship blog—*of course* I had been in love before. There was only one relationship that stood out from the masses of little flings, and for a time, he was my world. My ex and I met in college (although he wasn't in school—a sign of different horizons that would eventually be the pitfall of our short-lived romance), and we developed our own little cocoon, which quickly meant everything to me.

I had grown up with a happy home life, two parents who met, fell in love, and then stayed together. I had a naïve perspective that when you meet the right person you fall in love, and that's that. I never doubted him for a minute; this was what was *supposed* to happen. I trusted it, the process of companionship, and I let myself settle into having someone.

After only a few short months together, my boyfriend said he needed to move since he could no longer afford to live in Boulder, where I was going to college at the time, so we made the decision to move in together. Whether he meant for that to happen or not, I'm not really sure. I had more financial resources and was able to subsidize the move—a theme that stretched throughout the majority of our time together.

Our decision to move in together felt like every other decision we made—an initial excitement that then was held together by necessity. I have no other way to describe our time together but fearful. Fearful of being alone. Fearful that I had made a mistake. Fearful that if he left, it was because I was unlovable, that there was something wrong with me.

In retrospect, I had an anxiety that was speaking volumes, louder than my voice ever could. I remember sitting in a park alone, crying, before signing the lease. I knew, deep down, that there was nothing solid about our life together, but I didn't know what else to do. Truly, I thought this was as good as it was going to get.

Quickly claustrophobic by our limiting world together, he began to rebel against our relationship and me. Within a matter of months, things started to fall apart. He became angry and mean. I didn't know how to process this sudden shift and blamed myself. My life went from being my own to ours, to trying to salvage what was left in any respect.

I was quiet most of the time. My mom describes me as being very "proper" during that time, always quiet and trying not to say the wrong thing. As a woman who had built a life on being an outspoken, fearless thinker, I was quickly becoming a far cry from the person I once was. It was a strange time, and although I don't remember many of the details, I do remember it being extraordinarily painful. I had let myself and my old hobbies go, and I'd slowly begun rejecting a lot of what was still left of the old me. I became the enemy for both of us, it seems, since I seemed to be the cause of much of his anger.

My boyfriend told me incessantly that I was impossible to deal with, that I was impossible to love. He made his points clear. But I was lost in the world we'd built and didn't know of a way out. Eventually, after sitting in that toxic mess we'd built for too long, I ended it.

I was sad for a long time. I went back to being lonely, in an empty house, and I felt like a failure. To be fair, I was young. In the beginning, I suppose more than anything I was just excited not to be alone anymore. In many respects, I see now that I was taken advantage of. In most respects, I wasn't strong enough to stand up to my own fears and make good decisions.

Then, three years later, I met my current boyfriend, Chase. By then I was back to being strong and independent, with a great job and lots of dreams, friends, and a strong backbone in relationships. I had spent years processing how I had lost myself before, and I was determined to never go through that again. But then the strangest thing happened: I started to feel these feelings that I had never felt before. Unlike anyone before in my life, Chase loved *me*. And unlike anything in my life, I loved *him*.

I didn't just love the *idea* of him or the companionship of being together, but I adored the person that he was. He enjoyed the person that *I* was. And as I fell in love with him, they were feelings that were brand new. They were feelings of belonging, safety, passion, and companionship—and they didn't have an ounce of underlying fear.

I realized that for the first time in my entire life, I was really falling in love.

Sometimes in the beginning, and even still today, I'll become untrusting and difficult and attack out of nowhere. The naïve trust that I had so long ago got used up and beaten up by the wrong person. But, unlike that wrong person, Chase protects everything: my happiness, our life together, and my relationship with myself.

So if there's one thing that I learned the hard way in all of this, it's that there are two experiences we can define as love: we can fall in love with a person, or we can fall in love with companionship. When you fall in love with a *person,* you get to experience their companionship as a byproduct. When you fall in love with *companionship,* it becomes an arrangement of need, where you become hinged on losing one another. It's built on fear, necessity, and power. *And that isn't falling in love.* I can promise you that when you fall in love with a person, and they fall in love with you, you won't lose yourself in love—because you will be an important part of that love and what makes it tick.

After a year of dating, Chase and I are moving in together this summer. It isn't because we need to. It's because we've slowly become a family already, and a place together is an exciting next step. For the first time in my decorating-impaired life, I'm planning curtains in my mind and begging him to go to Ikea with me. This next step is an exciting leap, and there's no fear attached.

For the first time, I'm in love—and I haven't lost myself even a tiny bit.

BECOME YOUR OWN BIGGEST FAN

by Jenni Hanley

> *If you make friends with yourself, you will never be alone.*
> —Maxwell Maltz

When I was eighteen, I glided across the stage in front of my classmates to collect an award from the principal: All-Around Female. I was a dancer on the drill team; an officer in the a cappella choir; a youth group leader; a singer in the show choir; a member of the honor society, Spanish Club, and Venture Scouts; and top ten in my class. I wore these achievements like a shield, clueless of what or who I would be without them.

Inevitably, when I moved out of state for college, my shield cracked. There was no drill team, no honors points, no one to pat me on the back for working hard. I learned quickly that, when excellence is the default, it's a lot harder to stand out. With my shield in shambles, I had to search for a new persona—a new person to "be."

For some people, that might mean volunteering or learning to play an instrument. For me, it was making six or seven trips to the KFC buffet line, eating fried chicken and potatoes until my stomach hurt, and then throwing it all up at the nearest gas station. It wasn't pretty. But with no other labels to hide behind, it was comforting.

Every so often, I indulged myself in another label: girlfriend. It was so easy to melt into someone else, and it took the focus off me. Still, when I met Randy, I didn't see it coming. He was a young, compassionate pre-med student who was eager to complete me—and I was happy to let him. At first, it was a great arrangement. But after a year or so, the full weight of my unhappiness surfaced. I was jobless, directionless, and lonely; I came home to Randy every night, but even he couldn't fill the caverns I'd created in my life.

Making the decision to move back home and check into an eating disorder treatment center was difficult, but it was also the first decision I'd truly made for myself in a very long time. Getting physically healthy was the first step, but getting mentally healthy was the most important.

One day, the program director asked what my values were. I was stumped. *Student? Singer? Daughter?* I listed off an encyclopedia of labels I'd used at some point in my life, waiting for a nod of affirmation. But he stared back blankly.

"I'm not asking what you *are*," he clarified. "I want to know what's important to you."

I struggled with his question, trying desperately to reframe my life from this perspective. As long as I could remember, I'd been trying so hard to *be* one thing or another instead of just letting my life evolve organically. But as it turns out, I'm more than a student, an overachiever, a writer, or a girlfriend; I'm a young woman who values compassion, empathy, worldliness, and family. Painting that full picture of myself was a huge step forward.

But in my relationship with Randy, it was a huge step backward. Having finally learned that I could love myself and be complete on my own, there was no room for him. I began to feel physically sick when he tried to hug me. I didn't want him to touch me, or call me, or show me any kind of affection. He was the same kind person I'd always loved, but I felt claustrophobic. Slowly, painfully, I pushed him out.

That chapter of my life was debilitating and painful, but I emerged from it with a very important lesson: another person will never be able to compensate for the holes in your life. Be your own "other half," and seek a partner who will complement you, not complete you. As someone who had always sought external validation in the form of awards, activities, or relationships, this wasn't an easy lesson, but it's been crucial for me in the development of a richer, more mature self.

Do you ever find your features blurring into someone else's? Do you ever seek validation through compliments from others or likes on Facebook? It's easy to latch on to different identities when you don't fully understand what makes you uniquely *you*. It's a difficult habit to break, but it can be done.

The first step is to learn about what matters to you. Make a list of all the qualities you value in yourself: do you value charity? Is it your goal to travel the world? Are you funny? Driven? Patient? Things like your career, your car, or your body shape will come and go throughout your life. Uncovering the remarkable core aspects of your identity will make you less inclined to cling to external descriptors.

The next step is to accept responsibility for your life. One of the reasons it's so tempting to focus on the negatives we see in ourselves is that it provides a sense of control. If you're unfulfilled at work, complaining to others can provide a sense of validation. If you're frustrated that you don't travel as much as you'd like, rationalizing can be comforting. Stop making excuses and start making changes—starting with limiting comparisons. Obsessing over all the things you wish you had is one of the fastest tracks to unhappiness. I'm guilty of spending hours on Facebook or Pinterest, pining over a friend's new downtown loft or the hundreds of intricate recipes I don't have time to whip up every night. Consider giving yourself a social media allowance, like no more than five minutes of Facebook per day. It will really take the focus off others and put it back on you.

Lastly, learn to be comfortable being alone. When you're uncomfortable with solitude, it's easy to cling to others for validation of your worthiness. But what happens when the other person moves on? Relationships entered into out of necessity are bound to end painfully, because our needs change over time. When you learn to enjoy your alone time, you'll never *need* another person to fill the space.

When I first started this process a few years ago, I noticed I had developed a habit of deflecting the conversation from myself onto other people. When asked what my goals were, I'd tell everyone that I wanted to make my parents happy, or that I wished I had it together as much as so-and-so. My therapist at the time would always tell me, "That's her garden, stay in yours."

How can you ever grow a beautiful rose bush if you spend all day eyeing the tulips next door?

YOU ALREADY KNOW YOUR SOUL MATE

by Sheila Prakash

> *You, yourself, as much as anybody in the entire universe,*
> *deserve your love and affection.*
>
> —BUDDHA

Over the summer, my husband and I decided to take our lovely nieces and nephew out for a day of fun in the city. I expected a day filled with fun, laughter, and connection, but I was in store for much more—a lesson in love and truth from my eleven-year-old niece.

We were all at dinner and decided to play a game where one person asks a question of their choice, and everyone else answers. The question "Who do you have a crush on?" arose, and around the table we went. All the kids had normal answers, such as "um, Jason—no, Adam—well, sometimes Chris," "definitely Sarah," "I am not sure if I want to say," and so on.

Then the question came around to one of my nieces, and she answered with a big smile on her face, "Myself!" Wow, what an answer, I thought. If only I had that kind of wisdom and self-love at that age. I was so proud and happy for her that she saw herself through such a beautiful lens. Her answer started to make me think. How many of us have spent endless hours and years trying to find our true love, the one who will finally find us and make all that time we waited worth it—ultimately, our soul mate?

Could it be possible we have been searching for a connection that has been within us the whole time, as my niece pointed out? What if we took that term, "soul mate," and looked at it from my sweet niece's eyes. What would we see? Maybe we would see that a soul mate is not always someone else; it does not have to be outside of you. It could be the meeting of your soul and self within you.

Sometimes, we spend so much of our time waiting and searching for someone else to fill us up and love us that we forget how much love we already have inside that is patiently waiting to be released. We could find that missing piece if we turned inward and remembered how special and beautiful we are in our core. But, more often, we forget how to release this innate gift and fall into our own joy and divinity. We forget to connect to our power within ourselves. When this happens, we usually end up giving our power away and allowing someone else to define us. We allow ourselves to be seen through others' eyes, and eventually, we forget what we look like through our own.

If we search for our missing half, our soul mate, in another person, we inherently believe we are not complete without someone else. We convince ourselves we are not whole, and we can never be whole until we find our true love. I believe this false notion allows us to ignore our true potential and avoid taking responsibility for our own love and happiness. We end up using precious time trying to learn, accept, and love every possible mate, while dismissing the opportunity to learn, accept, and love ourselves.

Sometimes, we are quick to welcome all the "beautiful" and "good" aspects of ourselves, while avoiding the "bad" and "unacceptable" pieces within us. Would we do that to our true love, our soul mate? Or would we see and accept them for who they are?

I don't think we will ever be able to love ourselves until we acknowledge all our different aspects—the "strong" and the "weak"—and start treating ourselves with compassion instead of judgment. A puzzle needs all its pieces in order to be complete.

Now, I am not saying the only soul mate we can ever have is ourselves. I believe we can have different variations of soul mates, some being people who touch us profoundly and understand us deeply. But if we make a strong connection with ourselves, we will be able to live from a powerful, authentic place. From here, we will be able to identify our other soul mates more clearly because we truly know who we are and can see who inspires us to be more of our truth.

So, where do we find this amazing soul mate? I think it is the meeting place of pure divinity and humanness within us. Soul mate can be defined as the reunion of our lost self and found spirit. Only when we learn to love and accept ourselves are we able to receive love and acceptance from someone else. We must first feel it from within to understand and recognize it from without.

So, the next time you catch yourself wishing to be with that one person who could complete you and make your life perfect, remember: your wish could come true. You might just need to borrow my niece's lens so you can see more clearly. The mate of your soul is already here. It is you.

Top 4 Tips About Completing Yourself

1. **Use the mantra "I am loved" if you feel the urge to cling to other people.**

    Start recognizing if and when you feel a need to cling to people. Notice the emotions and fears you experience and recognize that you can change them. Researchers Mario Mikulincer and Phillip Shaver, who have studied what they call "security priming," suggest closing your eyes and visualizing the experience of being loved and cared for. Tell yourself, "I am loved," and you will slowly train yourself to feel the type of reassurance you're seeking from others.

2. **Challenge your fears around love so you don't end up settling for an unhealthy relationship.**

    Do you fear that being alone means you're unworthy? Do you fear that you'll lose your current relationship if you're honest about your desires or needs? Do you fear that you might not find someone else if you walk away from a relationship that you know isn't right? Fear—with its need, insecurity, suspicion, blame, and worry—is a barrier to genuine, unconditional love. Once you recognize your fears, you can challenge yourself to act in spite of them, one fear at a time, so that you can open yourself up to a healthy relationship when you're ready and the time is right.

3. **Identify your core values and priorities to better know, understand, and love yourself.**

It's all too easy to lose ourselves in relationships and blur the lines between us and other people—especially if we define ourselves in relation to them. Get clear on your top values and priorities, those things that create the foundation of your life and contribute to your sense of wholeness. That might include family, charity work, and time with friends. Now look at your current schedule. Are you honoring these things? If not, how can you start?

4. **Treat yourself as you want a partner to treat you.**

Are you looking for someone to compliment you, support you, and see the best in you? Are you waiting for someone who will love you unconditionally? Do you dream of finding a partner who will value you not in spite of your flaws and struggles, but because of them? Recognize when you do the opposite of this with negative self-talk and the choices you make, and then shine a light of compassion on your darkness, in the way you hope someone else will. This way you won't come to your relationships from a place of lack, with a void to be filled; you'll show up complete, prepared to give as much as you take.

CHAPTER 8

When You're Scared to Be Real: Allowing Yourself to Be Authentic

RESEARCHERS HAVE ESTIMATED THAT WE EACH SPEAK AROUND 16,000 words each day. But that number pales in comparison to all the things we don't say. We want to tell people when we're hurting, but we're afraid of looking weak and inferior. We want to share our dreams, but we're afraid of being questioned and criticized. We want to open up about our beliefs, but we're afraid of being judged and rejected. Deeper than all those fears is our need to genuinely bond with each other—not just on a superficial level, but based on our actual thoughts, beliefs, feelings, and even fears.

We need to feel deeply connected to other people, fully seen and appreciated by them, and secure in those relationships. We can have a million and one acquaintances, but if none of our connections feel intimate and meaningful, we will ultimately feel alone. There's actually some interesting research that shows we tend to value physical possessions less when we feel loved and accepted by others, because relationships can provide a sense of comfort, insurance, and protection. They truly are the most valuable things in our lives. In order to create these connections, we need to let our guard down—to stop worrying about impressing other people or avoiding their judgment, and show up as we truly are.

This kind of vulnerability can be terrifying, because you never know when you show someone your authentic self how they will receive it. You can't be certain they'll respect and honor your truth. You can't know that they will appreciate your perspective and offer you compassion and understanding. And you can't be sure that they'll respond to your openness in kind, sharing themselves with the same courage and sincerity. All you can know for sure is that the benefits of opening up far outweigh the disadvantages of staying shut down. Naturally, some people will stay closed off, but it's worth the risk of feeling vulnerable to find the ones who won't.

Still, so many of us limit ourselves from forming those deeply satisfying, close-knit bonds because we want to play nice, or fit in, or feel in control—or maybe because we have no idea who we really are. We're always learning, growing, and evolving, and it can be challenging to feel a secure sense of self when addressing the various parts of ourselves we'd rather change or deny—it's challenging, but it's not impossible.

If we make the effort, we can discover who we are beyond our roles and distractions. We can understand the feelings, thoughts, and needs that lie beneath our masks. And we can embrace both our darkness and light with an appreciation for our complexity and humanity. Countless Tiny Buddha contributors have addressed these questions on the site, sharing their experiences and insights. Some of those include . . .

THE PATH TO LIVING AUTHENTICALLY

by Julia Manuel

> *Don't think you're on the right road just because it's a well-beaten path.*
>
> —UNKNOWN

Growing up in Appalachia, women always had grace, class, and sweet iced tea in the refrigerator for unexpected visitors. They smiled when called ma'am or darling and kept an immaculate home. Many Appalachian women also abided by two rules: *it's impolite to say no*, and (my mother's favorite adage), *be as nice as you possibly can be, and everyone will realize you're the better person.*

For me, this translated as always say yes and play nice. I thought this equated to being compassionate and sensitive. What's that? You're stranded on the side of the road four hours away during an ice storm? I'll get you. You want to be intimate on the first date? I don't want you to dislike me, so okay. You think I'm hateful, unworthy, and a crybaby? You're probably right.

I played nice for so long that laughter turned to appeasement, confidence turned to tolerating harassment and verbal abuse, kindness turned to obligation. As I allowed others to treat me unkindly and without respect, living soulfully became impossible.

I always thought that I kept everyone at arm's length with a smile on my face because I didn't want to be hurt. In reality, I was so angry with myself for those specific moments of being run over that I willingly began playing the victim. It became easier to sabotage myself and continue down that road than to work hard and become a strong, outspoken, vivacious woman again—which wouldn't unfold until years later, after spending the night in the middle of nowhere.

In 2009, I left my Appalachian roots behind and hightailed it to the West Coast with my fiancé. But there was an unexpected pit stop in Marfa, Texas, population 2,000, where I changed course forever. Splitting the long drives cross-country, my fiancé slept as I descended onto this plateau of immeasurable prairie grass hemmed by stately mountains. The sunset was hypnotic, a brilliant rust so unfamiliar as it slipped off the horizon. There was nowhere to hide. I was breathless and exposed.

Sitting by the motel pool in the dead of winter, the urge to cry was unbearable. But I didn't know what to tell my fiancé, so I fought it. I was enraged, and for a long time I'd diverted my attention to blogging, drinking, eating, and sleeping; but in a one-horse town on a Monday night, the only people for miles are nuns, and I had to look at me.

I couldn't remember the last time I was truly happy and laughed genuinely. Once again, I was angry that I had deprived myself of that. Then a flood of memories came back when I was strong, truthful, confident, and beautiful. Those traits were still there. Standing alone amidst tumbleweeds and dust devils, watching the Marfa mystery lights with a thermos of bourbon, I finally heard myself. Never in my life had a physical moment connected so intensely with a spiritual one.

We resumed our drive the next morning, and I was exhausted. Once our cross-country journey ended in San Francisco, I didn't know how to be nice to my fiancé for two months, because my only thought was, "Who am I?" I was paralyzed. I spent every day huddled on the floor between the bed and the wall pouring over job ads, trying to find anything that would give me a role to fill. I had no idea how to be myself.

That moment of clarity in the desert ultimately led to rediscovery, which was uncomfortable. I wasn't leaving the apartment because all I had was myself, and I didn't know or trust that person. And one day, I rode a bus and ate alone in a restaurant for the first time in my life, terrified.

My year in San Francisco became the most humble year of my life. My clothes didn't even fill one dresser. I went from being a corporate guru to stocking the fridge in a law office. As cliché as it sounds, taking the unpaved back road on this journey and abandoning the familiar was liberating. My clothes fit better. I was glowing. My fiancé and I scraped by, but we were living in a gorgeous Edwardian apartment and eating amazing yet simple meals.

Indulgence was a scoop of ice cream or a good beer. Date nights were no longer extravagant dinners in ties and dresses, but walks to the park after work to find my fiancé on a blanket reading. Then, we would wander across the city for hours until we decided to call it a night. We didn't judge or expect anything that year, and we appreciated everything.

I knew that it would be hard for me not to fall into old habits once I moved back to Virginia. I am a yes man again, and the anger toward myself builds each day. I feel as though I scattered pieces of myself across the country—my heart in San Francisco, my freedom in Marfa—but that's not true. I know that I am capable of practicing kindness toward others and myself while being authentic.

I wrote to a friend after reading Baron Baptiste's *Journey into Power*:

I've been reading this book for a yoga workshop, and there was a passage about releasing yourself from the lies of everyday life that define you, and that you may not like who you really are at first, but at least it's true. I was so sad because I realized that's what happened in Marfa. I finally saw myself for the first time in many years and was mad at who I had allowed myself to become. At the same time, I was so happy and even scared to find "me." I think I'm longing for the day to come back or at least searching for a way to bring a piece of that here!

I'm now making it a point to live authentically. Being immersed in a yoga teacher training program has taught me a lot of techniques, one of which is to stop trying to win the Oscar. Essentially, stop playing roles. The first question people ask in the DC area is, "What do you do?" My answer is, "Hi. I'm Julie." This usually prompts, "Yeah, but what do you do?"

My next answer is, "Well, today I took the dog for a walk and had a nice nap." I've stopped being the consultant, the dog owner, the victim, or the gardener and started just being Julie.

The next step is to get rid of baggage. Once a month, I go through every closet and donate items I haven't worn or used in awhile. We tend to live excessively, and it's liberating to not let material possessions define you. Then, of course, there's getting rid of mental baggage through meditation. Even if I only have five minutes, I pull into the parking garage at work, fold my legs in the driver's seat, and close my eyes. Dropping the day's to-do list allows me to focus on the now.

Lastly, I make it a priority to stay connected with genuine friends. Real friends will be honest with how you land. I've started having regular check-ins with friends who will speak honestly about the energy I emit.

By the way, my friend replied to that email: "You will find a piece of Marfa if it is within you now." It is here, deep within my chest. It radiates soothing sunlight and power. It is beautiful and it shines.

BEING HONEST WITH OURSELVES AND REMOVING OUR MASKS

by Charlie Tranchemontagne

> *Our lives only improve when we are willing to take chances— and the first and most difficult risk we can take is to be honest with ourselves.*
>
> —WALTER ANDERSON

For almost two and a half decades, I hid behind masks. As a very young child I was my true self, like most children are; but as I got older, I started putting on masks as a way to fit in. One of my first masks was that of a juvenile delinquent. Over time, this mask became almost embedded in my skin. I discovered the world of alcohol, drugs, and mayhem, and I felt trapped and unable to escape from it. Shame and guilt filled me with fear and kept me from breaking free from this chaotic lifestyle. I was afraid to ask for help.

But in the late eighties, I attended a self-help workshop. This presentation introduced me to a way of living that radically altered my life—inner journeying. I was intrigued by the presenter's story and his thoughts of living a life that required him to look inside for answers. I had very little understanding of the concept or practice of looking within.

The workshop focused on removing masks, and it opened up a whole new way of living for me. As I listened to the speaker, I found myself thinking about my own life and the masks that I hid behind. I felt uncomfortable, so I started to question how I was living. This new self-awareness pushed me to start looking inside for answers to the problems that were plaguing me.

I was young and self-employed, on my way to making a name for myself in my business community. I was also absorbed with weightlifting and exercising. (I was the typical case of the skinny kid who transformed his body.) To others, my life looked good. But my inner landscape told a different story. I was lost in a world of darkness, pain, and anxiety. Even though I was experiencing some modest success with my business, my past was starting to haunt me. I felt like a fraud, and I was starting to feel like my outer world was about to crumble.

What kept me going through all these years of turmoil was the fact that I had become an expert on wearing masks. I had no idea who I was, and despite all the good things going on in my life, I felt like I wasn't being honest with myself. I wanted to be real.

When reflecting on what I could possibly share with others in regards to wearing masks, I immediately thought of a poem I read shortly after attending the self-help workshop. The poem, written by

Charles C. Finn, was titled *Please Hear What I Am Not Saying,* and it centered on the idea of wearing thousands of masks and being afraid to take them off. Finn's words seemed to tell my story, and I knew after reading his poem that I wanted to start changing my life.

Spending time reading new books and reflecting on my life in solitude did not come easily to me. I had to rearrange my priorities, which took practice. But as I spent more time reading and reflecting on the poem, my walls of resistance began to weaken. Light was starting to shine in some very dark places within me. My initial reaction was joy, followed quickly by fear. I knew I desperately wanted to change, but I felt afraid of the unknown.

When my masks started to come off, I felt like people could look right through me. I felt raw and naked. I did, however, experience a new inner freedom that was unfamiliar to me. My self-confidence rose along with my self-esteem, and despite the long road that lie ahead, I felt ready to start traveling it.

Presently, I am working on trying to remove a mask that has worn out its welcome. This is the mask that I started to wear shortly after I had a profound experience through skydiving. On October 8, 1990 I was sitting on the floor of a small Cessna plane, flying at an altitude of about four thousand feet. Resting on a small platform, with both legs hanging outside the door, I was seconds away from jumping.

What brought me to this crossroad was the fact that, despite appearances, I was still a mess on the inside because I still lacked inner peace. The workshop and poem had helped move me in a good direction, but I needed something more to push me over the edge. Skydiving would be that push. I had chosen to skydive as a way to surrender my life to a power greater than myself. I no longer wanted to endure the pain I was experiencing. I knew I needed help with overcoming this obstacle I was facing.

Sitting in the doorway of the plane was a surreal moment for me—one that would allow me to break through years of pain. At that moment before I jumped, I told myself, "Keep your eyes open," and with a silent prayer, I leapt from the doorway. In an instant, I knew with certainty that I would never be the same after this experience. Yet, as ecstatic as I was, I choose not to tell anyone why I had jumped. I thought it would be best to keep it to myself.

Up until that point, I had not shared my inner journeying experience with anyone. Religious or spiritual stuff still made me a little uncomfortable. I didn't realize that in not sharing this, I was hiding my true self—my "real" self. People around me knew that something was going on in my life, but I didn't disclose the driving force behind the changes they were seeing. It seemed easy just to keep things quiet.

So here I am, ready to take this "closet seeker" mask off. How do I do that? For me it is about finally admitting to myself that the mask no longer fits, and I am no longer willing to live this way. I wouldn't say that I have a "one size fits all" mask removal strategy, but I have found that when I am willing to step out of my comfort zone, good things will happen. I need to trust that.

I also know that self-honesty has a way of breaking through walls—big walls! What follows self-honesty, for me, is always action—taking some action, whether it's a small step or a giant leap. Either way, it's life-changing.

You may need to take a leap of your own to get in touch with your true self. It doesn't need to be huge, as long as you move forward in some way. Like Nike says, "Just do it." What's important is to find what works for you and start moving, inch by inch, beyond your fear.

Writing this essay is my way of trying to move beyond my fear, and removing this mask that has kept me isolated from other seekers. Most importantly, I did this to be honest with myself. Being honest with ourselves is the surest way to move forward on the path of self-discovery.

HOW BEING VULNERABLE CAN CHANGE YOUR LIFE

by Wendy Miyake

What makes you vulnerable makes you beautiful.
—BRENÉ BROWN

Vulnerability has never been my strong suit. It's no wonder. In order to be vulnerable, you have to be okay with all of you. That's the thing about vulnerability that no one tells you about. Being vulnerable is not about showing the parts of you that are shiny and pretty and fun. It's about revealing what you deny or keep hidden from other people. I bet you've never said to a friend, "Oh my god, I just love that I'm insecure." But that's the point of vulnerability, isn't it? You've got to love everything if you want to be vulnerable by choice.

Most of us have probably experienced vulnerability through default. More often than not, we are either forced into that state through conflict, or we are surprised by it after our circumstances feel more comfortable. Few of us consciously choose vulnerability because the stakes are too high. If we reveal our authentic selves, there is the great possibility that we will be misunderstood, labeled, or, worst of all, rejected. The fear of rejection can be so powerful that some wear it like armor.

My first real experience with vulnerability came when I was twenty-five. I had just accepted a position teaching literature to juniors and seniors in high school. This was quite possibly the most intimidating situation I had ever gotten myself into up to that point. We're talking teenagers here, the most extraterrestrial of all age groups!

To make matters worse, I asked my parents for advice. Being longtime elementary school teachers, my parents had a plethora of horror stories to share about unruly students, unreasonable parents, and teachers who could not control their classrooms. Each story ended with, "And that's why she quit and ended up going into retail."

I didn't want to be a quitter, so I listened well when they told me that I needed to be strong from the get-go, that I needed to show my students "who was boss." In the words of my father, "You can be a bitch and work your way down to nice, but you can't be nice and work your way up to being strong."

I took my parents' advice to heart. In the first week, I flunked seventy-five percent of my students on the summer reading exam. I yelled a lot to control the classroom environment. And when my students would complain about an assignment, I would say to them, "Remember, this class is not a democracy, it's a monarchy, and guess who's the queen?"

When I read those words now, I can't help but cringe. But at the time, I believed vulnerability was a liability. I was okay with being the dragon lady. It was safe. And under that façade, no one knew how terrified I actually was. So I wore that armor as if my life depended on it. If I had my way, I would have kept my guard up for the rest of that year. But my students were much smarter than me. They must have known on some level that, in the presence of true vulnerability, no one could remain closed off.

Perhaps no event demonstrated this better than when the senior honors project was in jeopardy. It was not traditional curriculum, and thus it came under scrutiny. My seniors were visibly upset because they had worked hard on their group papers, and they were looking forward to their presentations, where faculty from the high school as well as the local university would be present.

When my students expressed their feelings so honestly and openly, I could not turn away. I wanted to fight not only for the project, but also for the students themselves. When I thought we would have no choice but to abandon the whole thing, I remember telling my students that I wanted to quit. For the first time, I was very honest with them about how I was feeling and what I wanted for them. I was, perhaps, the most vulnerable I had been all year. And that moment of vulnerability paid off big-time.

When I left the school at the end of the year, I received many letters from my students. In them, I discovered that they were touched by the fact that I had fought so hard for them, that I was honest with them, and that I believed in them so passionately. At the time, I probably said to the universe something like, "Ah! You tricked me! This was supposed to be just a temporary job until my real life began. I wasn't supposed to invest in anyone or be committed to anything or care about anyone."

But I was very connected to these students long before I even knew I was. They eventually got to keep their senior project, but I received something so much greater. I learned what vulnerability looked and felt like. And I was the recipient of all its rewards.

Over the years, I have continued to experience that place of vulnerability. I cannot say that all my experiences have come through choice, but I do try to enter that state as much as I can. While I am far from being an expert on this subject, I have come to some conclusions that I hope will be meaningful to those who want to choose vulnerability.

First, vulnerability is so much easier when you love yourself. Think about it. When you don't love all of you and are afraid to show people the less-than-stellar parts, the space between you and vulnerability is like the Grand Canyon. You will need all the courage you can get to make the leap across. But when you love yourself, and I mean all of you,

you don't worry so much if someone else doesn't. And when you're less afraid of rejection, you step right into that place of openness.

Second, vulnerability takes practice. You don't just learn it once and then—ta-da!—you're easily open to everything and everyone. My experience at the high school was very profound, but even now, many years later, I still have moments where I'm more guarded and less willing to share the real me. Thank goodness life continues to give me opportunities to consciously choose openness. And most times, I do.

Third, the rewards of vulnerability are immeasurable. When I have chosen to be open, to show my authentic self, my students have met me there. And once we've formed that connection, there's nothing they can't accomplish.

With vulnerability you experience true connection—true love for yourself and for others—and you begin to attract people to you who are inspired by your openness. While it's not easy to be vulnerable, you'd be surprised how loving all of you and then sharing it with another can help you to connect with anyone.

In my own life, I'm continuing to open up to my students. I've been showing them a little more of the complexity that is me. They now know the ugly truth that I don't do math. They know that whenever I need to halve a recipe, my twelve-year-old nephew does the fractions for me. Shameful? Perhaps. But you know what? I like that girl—and in the end, so do my students.

HOW TO COME HOME TO YOURSELF

by Julie Hoyle

Man stands in his own shadow and wonders why it's dark.
—Zen Proverb

There was once a man who loved to complain and find fault with everyone and everything. Nothing pleased him, so he moved from one town to another, declaring as he left each place, "I am going to another town, where the people are friendlier."

A wise man perceived what the problem was, and as the angry man began striding along the dusty road to yet another destination, the wise man compassionately called out, "Oh brother, moving from place to place does not serve you well. Wherever you go, there you will also find yourself. Your shadow is *always* with you."

It took me a long time to understand that, in part, this was my story too. In early 2001, after taking a leave of absence from my job and arriving at an ashram in India, I anticipated the months there would be filled with experiences of light, peace, and expansion. However, within days I was assigned to work with a young woman who could be charming one minute and explosive the next. I was shocked and began pondering, "How could such an angry person be in this sacred place?"

Finally, after an episode of her screaming, purple with rage in response to the way I had handled a project, I realized it was time to take a deeper look at myself. Self-reflection took little time to reveal that there was anger, oodles of it, bubbling under the surface of my calm demeanor. Safely kept in check for as long as I could remember, the rarified energy of this meditative environment was revealing my long-lost friend, the "shadow."

For the first time, I began to recognize that this woman's anger belonged to me, and what's more, what I was seeing was just the tip of the iceberg. With this acknowledgment every hidden nuance of anger, in many glorious forms, began to surface. Frustration, despair, irritation, disappointment, and depression all came up for air after being hidden underground for so long.

During my time in India, I wrote in my journal, contemplated each experience, and asked the shadow to be revealed in dreams. I was also led to experiment with self-inquiry exercises.

One simple exercise went like this: write down the names of at least five people (living or dead) who inspire you. Beside each name, identify one positive quality they embody. For example, Mother Theresa: compassion. Acknowledge that in order to recognize these qualities, they must be in you. They are already "yours." Next, assume the direct opposite of each quality. For example, Mother Theresa: cold/uncaring. Take a moment to recognize and acknowledge that each "negative" quality must also be yours. Now ask, "How do you serve me?" and "What must I learn from you?"

When I gently asked questions to the cold/uncaring qualities, the responses were enlightening. I heard, "I serve you when you are not clear about your boundaries and take on too much. You must learn to honor your needs and know when to say no." In that moment, I realized that the shadow *also* contains positive qualities, and in order to be authentic, I needed to take ownership of both positive and negative projections.

Though simple, shadow exercises should not be underestimated. They are very, very powerful. They allow us to tap into energy that has formerly been repressed. Once released, a dynamic force initiates immediate changes in our consciousness and in our lives. What we are actually doing when we practice shadow exercises is re-establishing the studied qualities and the energy inherent in them in our psyche. Because of the power of the energy, this work is transformational. It can also be unnerving.

At its very core, the shadow is the collective name given to aspects of ourselves we are not taking ownership of because of fear. On a subconscious level, we are afraid that if people (or the community) "knew the truth," we would be judged, reviled, rejected, or worse, thrown out. As a consequence, we try to hide what we believe is unacceptable.

This pattern of behavior begins from the moment we are born. A normal aspect of growing up is that we are taught what constitutes appropriate social behavior and what does not. However, on a subtle or not-so-subtle level, we might also learn from our parents or caregivers that being creative is unacceptable, or that expressing moderate anger or frustration is going against the norms of society. When we internalize these messages, we form beliefs about what is "wrong" with us and repress them so deeply that they become unconscious. What we do not realize is that these aspects of who we are must find expression, and so we project them onto other people, organizations, or the world at large. This is how and why the shadow includes both all that we determine we dislike about ourselves and all the wonderful creative potential we are blind to being gifted with.

In addition, when we begin taking ownership of the shadow, we must also understand that this work is not about becoming someone else, or an "improved" version of who we think we are. Some people become addicted to becoming spiritual athletes, believing that if they meditate for longer and longer periods each day, endure fasts, and chant nonstop, they will attain enlightenment. While these practices are beneficial and supportive for stilling the mind, entering presence, and becoming aware of resistances, they are not "it."

Indulging in long hours of practices as a way of trying to fundamentally change who we are is often a camouflage for lack of self-worth or even self-hatred. What we must do instead is wake up to what we are repressing, own what we are "putting out there," and reclaim our inherent gifts, skills, and talents.

In support of this we can also ask: which gifts have I been neglecting? How can I start to make life choices in support of what I have to offer?

Ultimately, shadow work marks the beginning of the end and is a turning point on the spiritual path. In essence, we are electing to grow up and stop finding fault with everyone and everything "out there." Then, as if by magic, our natural state of unity consciousness begins to break through like the light of a new dawn, and we discover there is no longer a desire to keep running. We have simply, joyfully, and gratefully come home to who we really are.

Top 4 Tips About Being Authentic

1. **See yourself beyond your roles.**

   Ask yourself: Who am I? Then write a response stream-of-consciousness style that focuses on your gifts, strengths, interests, priorities, and passions. Resist the urge to list roles, like writer, mother, brother, runner, or yogi. Your roles in life will change—and the roles you currently fill may not be ones you chose based on your authentic wants. The goal isn't to define yourself; it's to get to know yourself—what you enjoy and value—as this is the first step in accepting and sharing who you really are.

2. **Take a tiny step to move beyond your mask.**

   You might be wearing a mask that conceals your true feelings, fears, and insecurities; or it could be a mask that reflects who you think people want you to be. Take a tiny step to move out from behind it. That might mean sharing something with a friend that you usually keep to yourself, or participating in an online discussion about something you formerly felt a need to hide. Once you experience that fulfilling sense of connection that comes from being authentic, you will likely be inspired to continue on this path.

3. Challenge yourself to be vulnerable.

It can feel safe to be guarded, since other people can only really reject us if they fully see us. Being guarded can also give us the illusion of control—if we believe showing emotion is a sign of weakness, then concealing it becomes a sign of power. But we never really connect with people when we try to manipulate their perception. Instead, we come to each other as shells of our real, multifaceted selves. Challenge yourself to be a little vulnerable. Admit if you feel uncertain. Reveal how much you care about something. When you release the façade and show up as you are, you reinforce to yourself that who you are is worth sharing.

4. Ask yourself, "What is my shadow side trying to tell me?"

Jot down five positive traits you wish to possess and then their opposites. Now ask yourself what the negative attributes might be teaching you when they're present in your life. For example, rudeness might be teaching you that you need to get more sleep so you're not so irritable; dishonesty might be teaching you that you need to value your needs, instead of giving people excuses about why you can't meet theirs. When you face your darkness head-on, you show yourself compassion, learn from the feelings or traits you're tempted to repress, and reduce your shadow's power over you, minimizing internal conflict.

CHAPTER 9

When You Don't Prioritize Self-Care: Taking Care of Yourself

We don't have the time. We have too much to do. Other people want and expect things from us. We make all kinds of excuses to avoid taking care of ourselves, oftentimes because we feel guilty or selfish putting our needs first. Particularly for women, we feel a strong instinct to put others ahead of ourselves. In her book *Revolution from Within: A Book of Self-Esteem,* Gloria Steinem suggests that we can become "empathy sick"—we can spend so much time trying to be there for others that we lose touch with what it means to be there for ourselves. We end up neglecting our needs, partly because we have no idea what they are.

But self-care is not just about overcoming guilt and fostering self-awareness—it's also about respecting ourselves, as we generally only protect and nurture the things and people we value. We have to believe our needs are important or else we won't prioritize them. We have to know that we don't have to overextend ourselves, sacrifice our interests, or prove that we're not selfish in order to be good people. And we have to know there's nothing wrong with having the specific needs we have. Until we stop judging our requirements for happiness, we will not be able to honor them.

Those requirements are different for everyone. Some people need more alone time, others, more socialization. Some people require more downtime, others, more activity. And our needs change over time, too, depending on where we are and what we're going through. Sometimes we need to push beyond our comfort zone; sometimes we need to cut ourselves some slack. Sometimes we need more time for contemplation; other times we need to stop thinking and get going. This means we have to frequently reassess what we require physically, emotionally, and spiritually; and we have to stay open to changes as we navigate new situations and challenges. Most importantly, we need to see self-care as an integral part of our happiness and fulfillment—something that enables us to be who we want to be, not something that lengthens our to-do list and prevents us from doing what we want to do.

Books and articles on self-care often suggest that we can't help others until we help ourselves and then reference the airplane instructions to secure our own oxygen masks before assisting others. I've also written these words. It's true that taking care of ourselves better enables us to support other people, but it's not just about increasing our ability to be good for others. It's also about acknowledging that we deserve to be good to ourselves.

How do we identify what we require in this moment for our overall well-being? Why do we feel so resistant when it comes to doing the things that we know are good for us? How can we communicate our needs to other people, particularly when they voice needs of their own? Countless Tiny Buddha contributors have addressed these questions on the site, sharing their experiences and insights. Some of those include . . .

WHAT IT MEANS TO TAKE CARE OF YOURSELF

by Cat Li Stevenson

> *Be gentle with yourself. You are a child of the universe, no less than the trees and the stars. In the noisy confusion of life, keep peace in your soul.*
>
> —MAX EHRMANN

A couple years ago, I realized that I had lived twenty-eight years without knowing what it really means to love and take care of myself.

In 2010, I took some wonderful trips, trekking and exploring Costa Rica, Bangkok, and Taipei. My husband and I bought a second home, and I fully engaged myself in the improvements and the creativity of decorating a fresh canvas. I ran several races, including a half-marathon, and finished well. I joined a swanky health and fitness club where I could take trendy aerobic classes. I was "taking good care of myself."

Life was good. I worked hard; I played hard. The end. That was the story I projected. But it was hardly that simple or fabulous. There was a whole lot of turbulence in my life that I was trying to fix externally.

My grandma—who became the closest female in my life after my mom passed away—moved back to Taiwan after living in the states for twenty-five years. Instead of sitting with the hurt, acknowledging how

I felt, I planned a trip. I reasoned with myself: "No worries, I'll visit her in Taiwan in a few months." I booked a flight and put a Band-Aid on the fact that my grandma would no longer be thirty miles from me but instead over seven thousand miles away.

My baby sister—who opened my heart more than I ever thought possible—left for China. Due to financial hardship, my parents had decided that it would be better for her to live there with her grandparents for a few years. I fought it at first but then subdued my feelings by validating that this was the right thing to do. I remember waving good-bye to her from the taxi with this creeping feeling of sadness and then just stuffing it away.

While traveling overseas, I became pregnant and felt so much joy. My heart grew ten times bigger. It was that same bliss and expansion I'd experienced with my baby sister. After seven weeks, we learned that there was no heartbeat, and we'd lose the little bean to the universe. I remember feeling overwhelmed by grief for a few days and then bounced back as quickly as I could. I was back at the gym running full speed a few short days after my surgery.

Back at home, I became very busy trying to lease our current house and move into the new one. I remember my mother-in-law expressing sincere concern for me. She said, "Cat, I don't mean to be hard on you, but you're doing too much."

I remember becoming irritated and defensive. I responded, "Don't worry about me. I know it seems like I'm always doing things, but I really do take good care of myself."

After all, I worked out six days a week. I ate healthy meals. I drank sixty-four ounces of water daily. I had girl lunches. I had weekly date nights. I scheduled massages when I was stressed. And on most nights I even slept a minimum of six hours.

I took good care of myself—on the outside. On the inside, I buried vulnerability. I played the resiliency card. I sought out quick fixes. And I convinced myself I was okay. I wasn't taking care of myself emotionally at all. Unconsciously, I'd placed "I'll deal with it later" labels on several situations as they'd trickled into my life, unplanned. Somewhere along the overachieving path of seeking perfection and always looking into the future, I lost myself when these labels accumulated. I managed to forget how to take care of my inner world. After neglecting what was really going on in my life, I ended up curled into ball in our bedroom corner, head buried in my knees, feeling a heavy amount of pain all at once.

Humans are amazing, though; we adapt, we heal, we are capable of growing stronger. When we acknowledge that changes, challenges, and hardships are there to deepen us, to remind us that we *do* get second chances, and that we are each made up of love, compassion, and healing, something remarkable happens.

With this new awareness, I ended 2010 with the promise to live differently. I made a decision to wake up each day, wholly, by connecting to who I am—to nurture myself from the inside out, to be with life instead of delaying it—and, in turn, my days started to become more inviting again.

In 2011, I traveled to connect instead of using it as an escape. I became a morning person and started each day with ample time for writing, reading, and practicing yoga instead of rushing into the office, fighting traffic, and always feeling behind. I found peace by journaling and peeling back layers to heal the hurt that was buried beneath instead of pushing it away.

I started acknowledging my accomplishments and mini-successes and celebrated with small rewards instead of rushing to the next best thing. I slowed down, simplified tasks, reduced my online time, and committed to less instead of doing, moving, and achieving, simply for the sake of it.

I felt. I embraced the sadness I'd been carrying with me and leaned into my fears instead of placing a patch on them. I listened to my body. I became a vegetarian and practiced mindful eating instead of counting calories and agonizing over whether or not I consumed too many carbs.

I chose to let go of the stories I kept replaying about the past and the worries I created for the future instead of clinging on to fear and anxiety. I practiced saying no to the commitments that didn't serve my values instead of saying yes to everything and shorting myself with each added responsibility.

I created sanctuaries—weekly time for me to relax and just be—instead of waiting for burnout before replenishing. I followed my intuition and listened to myself in meditation instead of thinking and overanalyzing to the point of exhaustion. I asked myself questions and allowed it to be okay that I didn't have the answers right away instead of being hard on myself for not knowing.

I began fully acknowledging the present in its entirety—every aspect, including the playful, joyful moments, and the uncomfortable, challenging ones. Suddenly, the world took on a different appearance—a kinder, more meaningful, more abundant and compassionate glow.

When we take the time to reconnect with ourselves, replace our fears with trust, and learn to let go of the things we cannot control, this is taking care. When we listen to our intuition, embrace all of our imperfections, and stay authentic to who we are, this is taking care. When we ground ourselves in the present and make mental space to find clarity, this is taking care. When we discover our interior barriers and find courage to dissolve them, this is taking care. When we learn to be gentle with ourselves, this is truly taking care.

When was the last time you acknowledged the feelings that are asking for your attention? How do you take care of yourself from the inside out so that you can fully experience life?

WHY WE FIND IT HARD TO DO THINGS THAT ARE GOOD FOR US

by Hannah Braime

> *Have respect for yourself, and patience and compassion. With these, you can handle anything.*
>
> —JACK KORNFIELD

I find it hard to do things I know are good for me, harder than anything else in my day-to-day life. Yoga, meditation, and journaling: these have all been invaluable tools during my personal journey; yet I have to will, and sometimes fight, myself in order to do them.

It's not that the activities themselves are hard (although yoga can be intense). It's the motivation, the internal debate that starts up every day that I struggle with. Afterward, I feel great, more in touch with myself and far more at peace. But to get there, it's a psychological mission.

I used to think it was just me—that everyone else sat down to these activities with an eager mind and an open heart—especially people who write about these things, like I do, and practice them daily, like I want to. The fact that I was less skipping joyfully to and from these activities and more dragging myself with gritted teeth left me feeling like a fraud, which meant I wanted to do these things even less.

Over time, I learned more about self-acceptance. I learned to accept that this was the way I am, and perhaps I will always find it difficult to sit down and do these things. Yet I still felt alone with my struggles, and therefore afraid to really talk about them with anyone else.

Last week, I was talking to a friend about challenges he was having with a course I run. He was saying he felt resistance, he didn't know why, and it seemed like everyone else found sitting down and doing the work a walk in the park. They could just do it, whereas for him it was a daily battle. That sounded familiar.

As soon as I wasn't trying to hide the resistance, as soon as I let myself talk about it openly, I could think more clearly about why I felt that way and what was behind that resistance. And out of all those reasons came the realization: the resistance is on my side, and sometimes it's just misguided. Here are the different types of resistance we may encounter and why:

First form: resistance to changing. When we engage in practices like journaling, meditation, or even exercising, we might feel a resistance to change. This resistance might conflict with a desire for healthy change—the desire that prompted us to start up that activity in the first place—but it has a very healthy grounding behind it: change can be scary. Change is about going into the unknown, while what we have right now is familiar and comfortable, even if we're not 100 percent happy with it.

Second form: resistance to what we might find. Sometimes self-knowledge can be like charting new, undiscovered land. You think you've explored it all, then you turn a corner and there are miles and miles of untouched terrain still to go. You have no idea what might be lurking under the rocks out there, and sometimes it feels safer to just leave it untouched.

When we engage in activities that are good for our well-being, self-acceptance, and self-knowledge, we risk relaxing our defenses and potentially finding out things about ourselves that we might not like. The most important part of self-growth, though, is learning to acknowledge and accept those things for what they are—and even feel compassion for them.

Third form: resistance to being nice to ourselves. It's often an unconscious core belief that we don't deserve to spend time on and be nice to ourselves. As an abstract concept, it's a no-brainer: of course people deserve to be nice to themselves. But when was the last time you consciously did this? Taking time to nourish our emotional and spiritual well-being, taking time to get to know ourselves better can be a real challenge even if we think other people deserve it.

If we were brought up in particularly critical households, if a lot of value was placed on our achievements over our happiness when we were younger, or if we grew up in environments where self-care practices were frowned upon or ridiculed, we might feel a lot of resistance to being nice to ourselves. It might conflict with the messages we received as children, which we felt we needed to obey to be loved. As adults, these messages are translated into core beliefs about ourselves, even if we don't apply them to other people. But, again, they are there to protect us, and although they might now be obsolete, they are still working to make us loveable to the people we used to depend on.

Fourth form: resistance to trusting a process. I have a mini-cynic who lives in my head and scoffs at my yoga, scorns my journaling practice, and says, "Really, aren't you above this hippy nonsense?" I keep telling that voice that "no, I'm not above this hippy nonsense," but it still pipes up to have its say.

Trusting a process—especially a slow process that might not contain any obvious lightbulb moments and requires time and patience—is difficult. We might not feel like we are in control; it could seem like we're giving our all and getting very little in return. I don't think I've ever had any major epiphanies in my personal development; instead of a cascade, I've experienced steady, slow drips. I can't think of any major changes that happened day-to-day, but when I look back on a few years ago, the difference is enormous.

Last form: resistance to our own humanity. I recently started a regular "morning pages" style of journaling (writing three pages stream-of-consciousness every morning) after a few months off. I was shocked to find that, although I started off my journaling session feeling very virtuous for having overcome my resistance, I became increasingly anxious while writing. I couldn't understand how, after years of practice, I could still be feeling anxious about journaling. "I should be past this," and "I should be self-accepting enough to not feel anxious when I journal," were the dominant thoughts that fed my anxiety further and created resistance to opening up my laptop the next day.

When we've been doing something for a certain amount of time, we can build up expectations around our performance. We expect ourselves to be self-acceptance ninjas, spreading peace and serenity to all we come into contact with. We expect those emotions on the "negative" end of the spectrum to disappear. But of course it's not like that. I get anxious, I feel resistance, and that's part of what it means to be me. It's part of what it means to be human.

An important part of my journey is learning to accept that those things might never change, and to have respect for my resistance and the many ways it is trying to protect me. Our resistance can be infuriating, frustrating, and downright inconvenient, but it's developed for very good reasons.

When we have respect for ourselves, with patience and compassion, we can handle anything—including resistance.

RECOGNIZE AND HONOR YOUR NEEDS

by Kaylee Rupp

The way you treat yourself sets the standard for others.
—Dr. Sonya Friedman

In what feels like a previous life, I was a serial dater. I looked for attention, validation, and identification in relationships. Each guy, however wrong for me, seemed like the perfect fit for my empty hand.

Maybe I hated being around his smoking, but I brushed it off and tried to breathe the other way. Maybe our conversations were dull, but I thought it'd get better. Maybe I cringed at being dragged to another party, but I went, because he wanted to see his friends. This pattern continued for years. I stayed in relationships that were clearly wrong for me, dated people I didn't understand and who didn't understand me—just to be in one. It wasn't until an insightful Zen class that I even became aware of the pattern.

As I cozied up in the gently lit room, hot tea in hand, surrounded by kindred spirits, the Zen master began the day's lesson: needs. Huh. I sipped the sweet jasmine tea and listened intently, totally blown away by what our instructor was saying. Needs? What are those? Seriously, they weren't even on my radar. But they should've been. Needs are personal prerequisites to happiness.

We don't learn to pay much attention to our needs beyond the basics of food, water, and shelter. Television advertisements, popular culture, and the desires of others dictate our "needs." But I'll bet that, on a soul level, you don't *need* a cooler car, a bigger ring, whiter teeth, or more parties. What *do* you need then? Answering this question can be one of the most powerful transformations of your life. It was for me.

After that class, I started paying attention to my needs; and very slowly, I began attending to them. I needed to embrace my introverted nature instead of ignoring it or boozing it out at parties every weekend. I needed alone time—space to dream, think, and be. I needed peace and quiet. Deep conversation. The freedom to spend a Friday night in without guilt.

At first, recognizing these needs was rough. I hated myself for having them; why couldn't I be like the other twenty-one-year-olds? Why did bars overwhelm me? Why couldn't I socialize with his rowdy friends? It drove me nuts. So for a while, I continued to ignore my needs. I thought I'd just override them with more wrong relationships and parties I hated. But eventually, I couldn't ignore them anymore. I came to terms with them. Being aware of my needs was making room for me to actually start taking care of them.

It took years, but I'm finally at the point where I'm comfortable with my needs—and making them known. I'm with a guy now who not only accepts but embraces my introverted nature, so I have time to write, be alone, and spend a Friday night with a book without ridicule. It's allowed me the space to be more authentically myself, making me happier and more available for all of my relationships.

Maybe you can relate. Do you shove your true needs aside to fit in with what you're supposed to want and do? Do you tend to the needs of others before your own? When was the last time you asked yourself, "What do I need right now?"

The first step in honoring your needs is recognizing that it's not selfish, weak, or dependent. Sometimes we feel this way because we think the needs of others should come first. But how can you be available as your best self for others if you're not taking care of you? When you're happy and taken care of, it's more of a joy than a burden to take care of the needs of others.

It will take some time to get over the negative ideas about having needs, so be gentle and patient with yourself through this process. Just remind yourself that we all have needs, and there's nothing wrong or greedy about having them. On the contrary, it's oh-so-right to take care of them! Recognizing and attending to your needs is part of being good to yourself.

At first, you might not be sure what your needs are. For many of us, they aren't even on the radar. So ask yourself: what are my personal prerequisites for happiness? Not what commercials or your friends are telling you. What is your soul telling you? Do you need more creativity, passion, fun? More time in nature? Less stress?

Once you've started discovering what your needs are, check in with yourself often. Are your needs being met right now? If not, how can you make that happen?

It's tempting to beat yourself up about your needs, like I did. But you can't change them, so why fight them? You might not like what you find at first; that's okay. You don't have to like something to accept it. Just remember that everyone's needs are different. Let go of expectations and embrace whatever comes up for you. This is really a part of accepting yourself for who you are. Your needs are highly personal—a reflection of your authentic self. Being real with your needs means being real with yourself. It means being authentic and honoring you and your whole human experience.

Once you know your needs, the next step is to communicate them to other people. This can be tough. We're afraid of looking selfish or placing burdens on others. Let go of this. By communicating your needs to others, you're creating a mutually respectful environment, one where they'll feel free to express their needs too. So really, telling people what you need is pretty selfless! Just be ready to hear and honor their needs as well. Communicating our needs requires and creates a great deal of respect and authenticity in our relationships. When you're honoring one another's needs, you're creating the opportunity for greater accountability and love.

The last piece of this puzzle is tending to your needs, and it's the most important part. This step also takes time. You don't need to do a radical overhaul; start small. If you're a closet introvert like I was, try saying no to one party invite and enjoy that quiet time—guilt free. Baby steps will build you up to the point where your needs become priorities. Before you start feeling selfish, remember: when you're practicing stellar self-care, you're becoming more authentic and available for your relationships.

I won't pretend that these steps are easy. They're not. It took me a long time to get to the point where I'm aware and taking care of my needs, and sometimes I still screw up. It's always a journey. But it's a journey that's so worth it. They always are, aren't they?

So embrace the challenge, honor yourself, and attend to your needs for greater authenticity, self-love, and presence on this beautiful journey.

SPEAKING UP WITHOUT BLOWING UP

by Stephen Light

You don't have to worry about burning bridges if you're building your own.

—KERRY E. WAGNER

"I aim to please. It's okay, no worries. Please don't worry, it's no big deal." These are some things I've said when interacting with others. The truth is that it wasn't okay, and it was inconveniencing me. But I could never voice this to people. What if they didn't like me? I was taught to be polite and to respect my elders, so I considered it rude to tell someone that what they are asking for or what they are doing is actually not okay. I also didn't want to create any unnecessary problems or conflict.

I always seemed to end up doing things I didn't want to do, or helping people with things that they should do themselves. I would get frustrated and annoyed and end up taking it out on those people who are close to me. Why did I do this?

I was sitting in an aisle seat on an airplane once when a man asked me if I wouldn't mind swapping with him. His friend was sitting next to me and he wanted to talk to him. The problem was that this guy's original seat was near the back and was a middle seat. I didn't want to do it, and yet I did. I reluctantly smiled and said, "Sure, no worries." I then sat in the middle seat on the flight between two very large passengers, feeling cramped and annoyed. This is when it all started going wrong.

It never rains but it pours. The passenger in the window seat wanted to go to the bathroom, so there was a lot of climbing in and out of the seats. I just smiled and said, "No problem." The meal cart arrived, and because we were at the back, they had run out of the vegetarian choice, so I had nothing to eat. I just said, "Not to worry." My bag was in the compartment above my original seat, so I couldn't just stand up and get my book. The guy next to me was reading the paper, and it was draped into my space. I couldn't really say anything, because, as you know, reading a newspaper in the confines of an airplane is difficult, and he was trying. The other guy next to me was hogging the middle arm rest. My justification was that he was a big guy and he was cramped. What a shame.

I was fuming inside because I did not stand up for myself and what I wanted. I started blaming the guy who was sitting in my original seat for how I was feeling. If he had just stayed in his seat then none of this would have happened. This was the story of my life.

The truth is, I was a people pleaser and didn't like others to be inconvenienced. I would rather be inconvenienced than have someone else have to go through that. I had learned from an early age to teach people how to treat me. I was teaching them that it was okay to take advantage of me because deep down inside I believed I was not enough.

My key insights that pushed me to change were:

- I did not like unnecessary conflict and viewed conflict as destructive.

- I did not value myself and my needs, and I saw other people's needs as more important than mine.

- I did not know how to speak up without blowing up.

I heard a simple statement that helped me realize that conflict is natural and a given: "Conflict is a natural disagreement resulting from individuals or groups that differ in attitudes, beliefs, values or needs." The world is full of conflict, and it will never go away. I just had to learn to deal effectively with it when it came up.

My inner emotional state needed to be able to handle conflict without taking things personally and getting upset. I started seeing conflict as good, as it allowed me to speak my truth. I learned that I was not responsible for how others felt about my choices as long as I was not being selfish or offending. I started standing up for myself, and my experiences shifted.

I had to realize that my needs were important, as they expressed my inner desires. If I wanted to start living a great life, I had to start living it for me. This meant making my choices real by voicing them. This did not mean that others' needs weren't as important. It just meant that I gave a voice to my needs, which I had never done before. This was not easy, as I had to change.

I wanted people to know what was important to me. I needed to be able to take responsibility for expressing my needs. I needed to change how I spoke. I wrote down all the things I used to say that put my needs second, and I wrote out a list of ways of expressing my needs so they were first. Then I practiced saying these statements, which made them real. A few examples include:

- "Actually, it really doesn't suit me. Is there something else you can try?"

- "I really would love to help, but unfortunately I have something else I have to do that is really important to me."

- "Please, may I ask that you respect my choices and don't try to make me feel bad because of them? I do care about you. This choice is for me."

People resisted this new me, and there were some people who didn't like it. But instead of rejecting them for not accepting me, I loved them harder. I just tried to make sure they understood that these were choices for me and not against them.

The result is I started seeing myself as being enough. When I recognized this and started behaving in this way, the world responded by starting to see me as being enough, too. We have to accept ourselves to be accepted by others, and we have to teach people how to treat us. We deserve to be treated like the amazing, beautiful souls we are.

Top 4 Tips About Taking Care of Yourself

1. Nurture yourself from the inside out.

While it's healthy to keep active—spending time with friends, doing activities you enjoy, and taking care of your body through exercise—these things are far less effective if you're neglecting your inner world to do them. Make a list of things you need to do for your emotional well-being—journaling, relaxing with your iPod, or practicing deep breathing, for example. Then schedule and prioritize them. Truly taking care of yourself requires you to work from the inside out.

2. Be gentle with yourself if you experience resistance.

Being hard on yourself won't make it any easier to do the things you know are good for you. All this does is create unnecessary stress. Instead, have patience and compassion for yourself. Recognize that your resistance is trying to serve you, even if it's misguided. Once you stop blaming yourself and beating yourself up for struggling, it will be easier to learn from your resistance and then work through it.

3. Make a list of your top needs.

What do you need to feel emotionally balanced? What do you need to feel connected to yourself? What do you need to feel physically well? Get it all down on paper, without judging it or comparing it to someone else's needs. You may require a good amount of alone time for introspection, or social time for connection, or time to engage in your hobbies and passions. Once you know your prerequisites for happiness, you can design a life that honors them.

4. Practice saying no when a request would impact your ability to take care of yourself.

Other people will always have requests. You will inevitably feel resentful, not to mention depleted, if you expect them to anticipate your needs and help you honor them. While it may feel selfish to say no, it's actually a kind thing to do. The better you take care of yourself, the better you'll be able to help them—when and how you're able to, without compromising your own needs.

CHAPTER 10

When You Don't Feel You Make a Difference: Believing in Your Worth and Discovering Your Path

THERE'S AN INVISIBLE THREAD THAT CONNECTS OUR FEELINGS about ourselves with our feelings about our lives. The two are inextricably linked. We need to value ourselves or we'll never feel that our efforts are valuable. We need to have faith in ourselves or we won't have faith in our choices. The good news is that strides in one sphere can instantly affect the other. When we work on feeling good about ourselves, we feel better equipped to do things that we'll feel good about. When we do something we feel proud of, we naturally feel prouder of who we are. The beauty of this cyclical nature is that we don't need to wait one more moment to start doing something positive with our lives. Even if we go through times when we don't feel positive about ourselves—and we all inevitably do—we can each choose right now that we can make a difference in the world. And it can make all the difference in how we see ourselves.

We naturally feel more self-assured when we feel like our lives matter—that we're doing meaningful things that will help other people and the world at large. But it's not just about the impact we make; we want to feel purposeful, passionate, and blissfully alive. We want to love what we do with our days. If you don't yet know what would facilitate that, you can easily feel discouraged. You may feel even more disheartened if you know what you love but have no idea what to do with it—or if it's possible to do anything at all. It's a great big world with a lot of people working toward varied goals. It's all too easy to convince yourself there's no room for your talents and dreams.

You could get bogged down in self-defeating thoughts that paralyze you from taking action. You could put pressure on yourself, stressing about the big things you're not doing, wondering what you could possibly try that might feel good enough. You could feel overwhelmed by everything you don't know, and regretful about all the days you previously spent doing things that felt meaningless.

Or you could decide that what really matters is that you do something, anything, today that makes you feel good about you. You could explore, try different things, and use your sense of self-pride and self-satisfaction as a compass to guide your next steps. Even one tiny step in a direction that feels purposeful has immense power to change your perspective on yourself and your life. It might seem like fulfillment lies in the outcome, but once you feel the satisfaction of acting with purpose and passion, you'll realize the real joy is in the doing—enjoying, getting lost in a moment, and sharing that with others.

How do we identify a path that's right for us? How can we live up to our full potential? How can we change our lives for the better, and feel good about where we are right now? Countless Tiny Buddha contributors have addressed these questions on the site, sharing their experiences and insights. Some of those include . . .

CHOOSING THE RIGHT PATH FOR YOU

by Madison Sonnier

> *Your outlook on life is a direct reflection on how much you like yourself.*
>
> —LULULEMON

"My existence on this Earth is pointless." That thought crossed my mind every night before I fell asleep.

It had been several months since I graduated from high school, and I had no idea what I was going to do with my life. My future plans were falling to pieces, and everyone around me kept telling me that I needed to start accomplishing things that I had not yet accomplished.

I was not where I thought I should be in life. Everyone had expectations that I hadn't met. I became too focused on becoming a version of myself that everyone else wanted, and I constantly compared myself to other people who had already taken the dive into the next chapter of their life.

People relentlessly questioned, and, I felt, judged me for my slower progression in life, which convinced me that no one supported or believed in me. I began to blame everyone around me for the state of misery I had fallen into. My self-esteem began to suffer as the months went by. I felt inferior to everyone, and it made me hate myself. I still did not know what I wanted to do with my life—and I was starting to not even care.

But several months and hundreds of needless self-judgments later, I decided to block out the negativity, both from myself and other people. I silenced the voice in my head that told me I wasn't good enough and asked myself what would really make me happy.

I've always been creative and expressive. I used to sing, act, and dance when I was younger. But my favorite thing has always been writing. Some of the happiest moments in my life came from opportunities to express myself or put my heart and soul out for everyone to see. Every path I tried to take always led me back to writing.

I got to a point where I realized that I was only trying to pursue other paths because I thought that's what other people would accept. I was afraid that if I let my imagination soar to all the different possibilities, people would tear me down or tell me to be "realistic." I became paralyzed with this fear of not being accepted. I was afraid to be different or go my own way and pursue what truly made me happy. I'd put myself in a box.

One day, I decided that enough was enough. I had spent an entire year of my life trying to conform to other people's expectations, and I realized that you can't please everyone anyway, so trying would definitely not lead to contentment. Real happiness comes from being content with and proud of *yourself.*

I finally decided that I was going to devote my time to learning about writing and working on my writing skills. I am happy with that decision, and I feel better about myself because I made it for me.

I have learned a few things about choosing the right path for yourself and focusing on what will make you happy. The first thing is to try to let go of worries. They put a burden on your mind, body, and spirit. They can keep you up all night if you let them. Find comfort in the fact that everything happens for a reason, and everything will fall into place at the right time.

The next step is to stop trying to impress other people. The persistent need to please and compare ourselves to others is one of the most common causes of self-loathing. As long as you're trying to live up to other people's expectations, you will not please yourself. Happiness does not come from pleasing other people. Happiness comes from feeling content with your own life and goals.

Remember that everyone is different. Figure out what you're good at and what sets you apart from everyone else. Your mission is to create a reason for being here. When you start to figure out what you want in life, there will be obstacles. Don't let anyone or anything discourage you from continuing on. Believe in yourself and believe in your decisions. Stay positive and keep moving forward.

It may take you a while to figure out what you want. Take your time. I used to think that I needed to be at the same level as everyone else my age. Life is not a race or a contest, and it doesn't come with a rulebook for accomplishing certain things. Trust that you are exactly where you need to be at this very moment in time, and as long as you're content, don't let anyone convince you that you're *not* where you need to be. You be the judge of what you want to change in your life and then do it for *you*.

Lastly, surround yourself with positivity. Try to limit the amount of time you spend with people who naysay, judge, or ridicule. Choose to completely surround yourself with positive, inspiring influences. You will feel much happier and better about yourself if you do.

Finally, the most important thing to remember is that you *are* worth it and you *can* be happy. Life will not throw you anything you cannot handle or overcome. Once you start to accept and love yourself and your desired path, the smoke will clear and you will breathe easy again. Be kind to yourself and life will be a whole lot brighter.

LIES THAT PREVENT US FROM LIVING UP TO OUR POTENTIAL

by An Bourmanne

And in the end, it's not the years in your life that count. It's the life in your years.

—ABRAHAM LINCOLN

I used to think that I would motivate myself to really live up to my full potential by reminding myself how much I wasn't. Well, that didn't work. Not that I didn't get any results from chanting, "You are so not living up to your full potential!" while getting out of bed, combing my hair, doing the dishes, and driving to work. Any time was a great time to remind myself. So I didn't waste a second doing just that. And I got results. Only not the ones I expected.

I became an expert on mindlessly browsing the web and constantly comparing myself to other people. I became an expert on feeling stuck. I became an expert on driving myself crazy with my nonstop "you are so stuck" chatter in my mind. I felt drained, stuck, and low on energy; those were my daily companions. So it shouldn't be any wonder that I grew less and less fond of my so-called motivational mantra, which was doing anything but, well, motivating.

I've realized that living up to our full potential starts with eliminating three big lies.

First lie: it's productive to beat ourselves up about not living up to our potential. When we spend all our energy telling ourselves we're not doing well enough, we have very little time and energy left to look inside. Don't get me wrong, I was very busy. I was busy searching for my full potential. I read tons of books. I completed lots of quizzes to find my true talents and the right job for me. I browsed the job section of newspapers. I looked at what other people were doing.

In short, I was looking *everywhere*—except inside. I wasn't paying attention to what gave me energy. I wasn't paying attention to what fascinated me. Instead, I was writing the pros and cons for potential jobs but reaching a dead-end time and again as I failed to neatly add and subtract all the items from both columns into one overwhelmingly clear answer.

I've come to believe that we already know what leading a rich, meaningful, purposeful life means to us. It's just a matter of paying attention and listening to ourselves. It's taking action and checking in with ourselves to discover what feels good, what energizes us, what feels bad, what drains us, and what fascinates us. It's allowing ourselves to explore and experiment, one tiny step at a time. And adjusting where needed, using our energy levels and our fascination as a compass to guide us in creating an energizing, brilliant life that inspires us.

Second lie: living up to our full potential means living a life free of fear, failure, and sorrow. I convinced myself that living up to my full potential meant living happily ever after, in some kind of perpetual state of bliss. I've come to believe that this is a myth. Living up to our full potential means feeling the fear and doing it anyway. It means making mistakes and learning from them.

Living up to our full potential means seeing things as they are, not the way we think they should be, and taking action from that place. It means allowing ourselves to feel the way we do, not the way we think we should feel. It means diving in and exploring *why* we are feeling the way we do. That's when we find our answers. That's when we reconnect with our full potential. That's when we start tapping into our brilliance.

Third lie: we're not good enough. When we tell ourselves, "You are so not living up to your full potential!" we're basically telling ourselves, "You are not good enough the way you are right now." And that is such a disempowering lie.

I've learned that it is my choice whether or not to believe that lie. It is my job to let go of that lie and choose an empowering perspective instead. I've learned that I can make that choice every minute of every single day.

I'm being the best me I can be, right here, right now. I'll be thriving tomorrow thanks to the mistakes I am willing to make today. Living up to our full potential is not trying to avoid making mistakes. It's giving it our all, wholeheartedly, with everything we've got.

I am now reconnecting with my full potential through everything I do. I choose to do my thing, one tiny step at a time, at my pace, in my own fabulous, imperfect way. Some will like it, some won't. Living up to our full potential is being cool with that instead of trying to please everyone else. Living up to our full potential is giving ourselves permission to be who we are and tapping into our unique selves. Unapologetically.

I feel empowered, scared and excited, proud and determined, playful and inspired; these are just a few of my new daily companions on this long, fascinating, winding road that is living up to my full potential. And they didn't come into my life by accident. I chose to invite them in, one empowering thought at a time. And so can you.

STOP WAITING FOR LIFE TO HAPPEN AND START LIVING IT NOW

by Patrycja Domurad

> *The grass is always greener where you water it.*
>
> —UNKNOWN

For a while there, I was a little peeved with the world. I've just recently snapped out of it, and I just want to sing and dance and share this message with everyone: stop waiting!

Last year, after living through some profound experiences—traveling extensively, soul searching, attending incredible life-changing events, shedding massive masks, overcoming huge obstacles, and deciding to change the course of my life completely—I came back to my life, to my home, and sat back and thought to myself, "This is what life is about!"

I was on a snowball-effect high of massive changes. It was the most intense feeling that seemed to go on endlessly, and the changes just seemed to keep on unfolding in my life naturally, organically. I dropped out of a program at school I wasn't really committed to, with the intention of going to culinary college after a year off. I faced the world for the first time, trading in my signature sunglasses for an eye patch, after hiding a facial difference I sustained from a car accident almost a decade ago. I returned to my yoga practice, focused on my health and vitality, and dropped thirty pounds.

Last year was amazing, and it just seemed to keep getting better. I landed an amazing job at the company I was dying to work for during my year off before returning to school. I met amazing people and seemed to attract great new friends into my life. I traveled more for personal development courses and seminars and soaked up the amazing atmosphere that is unique to Tony Robbins events.

Around Christmastime, I began to sense a shift in myself and tried to brush it off. It wasn't much; it's just that it was no longer effortless to be happy, and I began to feel a little forced at times. Some challenges at work arose, and I was beginning to think that there was something wrong with me. After months and months of work that flowed easily, I began to realize that the wheels of my life weren't moving all too smoothly anymore.

At that point, I started to retreat. I had huge goals, big dreams on the horizon for the year, and it scared me when things weren't progressing. I began to take on a passenger mentality in my life, making excuses for my inactions and myself. When things got worse in any area, it was a huge blow to my self-esteem, and I let it break me down.

In January I entered what I consider to be a "winter season" of life. I got fired from the job that I loved, despite what I thought were my best attempts. I stopped going to the gym because my fitness goals were tied to my identity at work. I stopped practicing yoga for fear of running into ex-coworkers, and even began to dislike practicing at all.

After being so happy and wanting so many amazing things to come into my life I felt ashamed to be in a place where I had failed. I let that sense of failure eat away at my spirit, and I became defeated in the worst possible way. I didn't want to listen to anyone or anything. I became annoyed with my friends who were going places in life. I was annoyed with myself especially for believing in hogwash and thinking that changing your life actually lasts.

The truth is, I was waiting. I was waiting for something to come and shake me, wake me up out of that funky state. I was waiting for life to knock on my doorstep and say, "Here! I've delivered your answers! Ta-da! Easy way out!" I was waiting for things to stop being so difficult, for things to ease up on my plate, for things to miraculously get better, because it felt like a lot was happening to me.

I put the weight back on. I avoided friends. I didn't do anything really. I worked part-time, but whenever I wasn't working I was sure to drown any real thoughts in mindless television. I stopped writing. I avoided creating my daily gratitude lists, because they would inevitably become hateful rants. The memories of the year before and all of those amazing accomplishments seemed like someone else's.

After much reflection and finally taking ownership, I am happy to say I am standing on higher ground today. It wasn't easy to snap out of it. In fact, I made sure it was hard. When my boyfriend, the closest person in my life, finally called me out on my behavior and provided a harsh but necessary reflection to where I had led my life, I broke down. I avoided the accusations with an angry response initially, but I began to journal frantically when I realized the pain I was living with was self-inflicted.

It was then that I realized that taking ownership of my life also meant I had the power to change it. The more I wrote, the more I discovered about what I wanted. I had to face the things I didn't want to face in order to create a roadmap for myself. That is the thing about life: it gets hard. Things go awry. You get fired. You fall out of pace sometimes. You end up eating a pound of chocolate. So what?

Then I remembered this question someone once posed to me: what if life didn't happen to you, but happened *for* you? What if I examined all of the crap that had happened "to" me before and saw where it had led me? What if I realized there was a purpose for every circumstance of difficulty, struggle, pain, and trauma? How would my perspective change if I realized my quality of life is directly related to my reactions? Would I stop and appreciate these moments of darkness if I realized they are necessary to guide me to the light in my life?

With a change in focus, you can change your life. If you're looking to change your life too, realize you have the power to do it. Instead of waiting for life to happen, make it happen. Instead of waiting for a change, create a change. Create a vision for yourself and your life and use the opportunities that come when life throws you a curveball to review your goals and dreams. You may discover a speed bump was a wake-up call to focus on something important you may have otherwise overlooked.

What do you do on a regular basis? Who do you know? How do you feel? How are you awesome? How is your life incredible? What excitement, adventures, and amazing experiences have you had? Where have you been? What is something that you once enjoyed that isn't in your life today? Where do you see yourself in six months, in the most important areas of your life?

Now draw it in to three months: what needs to happen three months from now to get to your vision? Be specific! Are you trying something new? Have you changed your daily habits? What do you fill your time with? What is it like to be this awesome you, three months from now?

Hone in, one month from today. What is different? What steps have you taken to this new you six months away? What are you up to? What have you accomplished? What are you working toward? What have you consistently been doing for the past thirty days?

What happens to you a week from now? In seven days, how have you changed your habits and your life to steer its course to something new and incredible? What are you planning? What is being implemented? How do you feel?

Now plan tomorrow. Repeat daily. Plan your time, because time flies, but the good news is you're the pilot of your life. Stop waiting for life to happen to you and take ownership for leading your life. You have led your life to amazing places already, and there is no stopping where you can go from here.

RECOGNIZING HOW FAR YOU'VE COME

by Joanna Z. Weston

> *Always concentrate on how far you've come, rather than how far you have left to go.*
>
> —UNKNOWN

It is laughably easy to forget to stop and take stock of how far we have come in our lives. Our world focuses so much on what we lack—be it money, beauty, prestige, or romantic success—that it is far too common for us to get trapped in the loop of needing to have, be, or do "more" before thinking that we might be good enough. I, for one, do it all the time.

A year and a half ago, I was unemployed with no idea what to do next. I'd spent my life until that point ignoring the conviction that there was something I was meant to do. Since I didn't know what that calling might be, I played it safe by getting a library degree. I was pretty good at library work, but I was never passionate about it, which made me an unremarkable candidate for the few remaining library positions after the economy crashed.

All of this left me sitting at home, miserable. Unemployment, combined with a particularly nasty winter, led to a terrible flare-up of my lifelong nemesis, depression. To say that I was despondent that winter would be a gross understatement. Of course, I can now see that this was a blessing. That terrible winter pushed me to realize that something had to change, and fast. I was finished playing it safe and ready to figure out my dream!

Since then, I've identified my true calling to become a life coach, sought training, and now I stand on the cusp of living my ideal life. But is that always how I see the situation? Of course not. On many days, I find myself focusing on how far I still have to go. I see the programs I haven't implemented yet and the website that isn't quite perfect instead of taking the time to marvel over the fact that I have so many ideas and a website at all. And you know what? Failing to acknowledge how far I've come robs me of a lot of joy and a lot of pride. I may not have everything figured out in my new business, but I've come a long way from where I was a year ago.

I would be willing to bet that you've made huge progress in the last year as well but are too focused on what remains to be done to see it. I invite you to start giving yourself credit for a lot of hard work and achievement. Start by stepping back and taking a deep breath. It's hard to hear the truth when a thousand voices and worries are circling through your mind. Taking just five minutes to sit down and let the voices become quiet can make a huge difference.

From there, ask yourself, "Where was I this time last year? Five years ago? Ten? I can guarantee that you will be surprised by your answers. Change comes slowly, so it can be hard to see it, but it's always happening, whether we notice it or not. If you keep a journal or blog, reread some of your old entries. You'll find written evidence (in your own hand!) of just how far you've come when you see what was upsetting you back then.

It may also help to make a list of your own accomplishments from the last year or the last five years. I don't care how small or insignificant an event seems—write it down! Then look at that list and reflect on just how much you've done. You may want to ask a friend or loved one for input. We can be our own worst critics, so sometimes those close to us have a clearer view of how much we've grown than we have of ourselves. If it feels awkward to ask someone to tell you nice things about yourself, offer to return the favor. Remember that not all progress is related to your career. How have your relationships, your spirituality, or your self-knowledge improved?

As you go about your day, try to notice when you take even the smallest step toward your goals, and be sure to honor that in some way. Even just writing it down in your journal will give you that moment of recognition.

Most importantly, realize that it's never all done. We all want to reach the top of the mountain and feel that we have achieved something. We want to be finished, but that's never going to happen; our lives are a constant work in progress, which is the way it ought to be. Trust me, you'd be bored if you weren't constantly changing and growing.

Whatever you are working toward, and however far you still have to go, I encourage you to take the time to truly bask in everything you have achieved thus far. It doesn't matter if you are moving fast or slow, only that you keep moving! And the best way to ensure that you continue to do that is to cherish each step along the way.

Top 4 Tips About Believing in Your Worth and Discovering Your Path

1. **Ask yourself, "What would make me proud of myself if I weren't trying to impress other people?"**

   Forget about what you think people want you to do, or what you think you should do. Forget about appearances and what you think looks respectable or admirable. Forget about the pressure to do something important or big. Instead, ask yourself: what makes me feel good about myself? What activity always makes me feel passionate, purposeful, and proud? If I didn't have to worry about where it was leading, what would I feel good about doing every day?

2. **Experiment with what gives you energy.**

   Not everyone can answer that first question. If you can't, give yourself time and space to explore. Resist the urge to tell yourself that you *should* have things figured out by now. This uses up energy that you could otherwise use experimenting and paying attention to your instincts. Also, don't worry about making the "right" decision. Give yourself permission to try different things and see what gets you excited. You may not know today, tomorrow, or even a year from now what path feels right for you. But you will learn what *doesn't* feel right—and that's part of the journey to discovering what does.

3. **Create a vision and take tiny steps toward fulfilling it each day.**

What change would you like to see in your life six months down the line? What passions or hobbies do you enjoy regularly? What new habits have you adopted? What relationships have you nurtured? Now identify the first steps that will help you create those changes, and do one small thing each day to work toward those goals. If you're going through a difficult time right now, realize this isn't the end of the world; it's the beginning of a new part of your journey, and the perfect opportunity to evaluate what you want to change and how you can do it.

4. **Look back at where you were ten years ago, five years ago, and one year ago to celebrate how far you've come.**

It's all too easy to focus on everything you think you're doing wrong. Instead, take a moment to recognize everything you've done right—all the ways you've learned, grown, and improved over the last one, five, ten years of your life. Then tell yourself that your worth has nothing to do with those improvements. Life is about change and growth, but that doesn't mean there's something inherently wrong with who you are right now. You will not be the same person tomorrow as you are today—but each perfectly imperfect version of you deserves your love and respect.

CONCLUSION

THROUGHOUT OUR LIVES, WE'LL EACH EXPERIENCE OUR DAYS IN many different ways. We'll feel scared, lost, and saddened about the road behind us. We'll feel passionate, exhilarated, and eager to travel the path ahead. We'll feel paralyzed with fear and uncertainty, unsure that our actions matter. We'll feel energized with hope and possibility, knowing full well they always do.

It's the same for all of us. We each live a constantly evolving experience, with highs so immense it may feel like flying, lows so deep it may feel like dying, and limitless shades in between. This is what it means to be human, for all of us. Loving ourselves won't change that we won't always love what's in front of us. It will, however, change how we treat ourselves in response to it and what we believe we can do with it.

Loving ourselves means knowing that we are the constant in all our experiences, and that's something worth appreciating. Because each of us has a powerful light that we can use for so much good. Somewhere underneath everything we've learned to doubt or detest, there's a formidable force of strength and beauty—a spark so bright it can light a path through even the darkest days, not only for ourselves, but also for others.

To access it, we need to look back at where we've been and choose to see our pain as fuel for strength and wisdom. We need to know that our imperfections are gifts, not curses, for without them there'd be no individuality, no journey, and no opportunities to help others who can relate. We need to see our mistakes as tools to keep moving forward—not the building blocks of who we are but rather steps to who we can become. And we need to see ourselves as the beautiful blend of both our strengths and weaknesses. Even if others choose to focus on the latter. Even if we're tempted to think they're better than us. Even if we're afraid they might not value us when they see us for who we really are.

Every time our heart beats, we have a choice that can change the meaning of that beat: we can choose to see the worst in ourselves or decide to nurture the best. No matter where you've been, what you've done, or how many years you've lived, this second can change your life if you use it to believe in yourself. Because once you decide to believe—once you shift your perception from regret over who you've been, to faith in who you are—you dramatically change the potential of who you can be and what you can do. You transform your experience of every moment that follows. Instead of blaming yourself for everything that feels wrong, you start empowering yourself to create something that feels right.

This doesn't mean you'll never feel down on yourself. It doesn't mean you'll always feel confident and self-assured. It doesn't mean you'll always bounce back from failure, disappointment, or heartache with an immediate sense of optimism and hope. It means you'll eventually find your way home to a soothing place inside yourself, where your own thoughts and beliefs reinforce that you will be just fine. It means you'll know more and more every day that no matter how you struggle, you deserve to enjoy as many of the moments as you can.

If ever that seems hard to believe—if you have trouble accessing your faith in yourself—remember you're not alone. Whatever you're going through, take comfort in knowing that someone else has been there, is there now, or will be there someday down the road. We're all in this together. Today, one of the people who shared a story in this book may have been helpful to you. One day, you may be there to shine a light for them, or possibly for me. We're all doing the best we can, for ourselves and each other. As someone who formerly spent years believing that I wasn't good enough, I propose we each decide that's something to be proud of.

THE TIPS

1. Tell empowering stories of healing in the present instead of sad stories of hurting in the past.

2. Challenge the limiting beliefs that make you feel bad about yourself.

3. Shine a spotlight on your shame and douse it with empathy.

4. Recognize the beauty in your journey.

5. Identify what feelings you've been trying to outrun or numb.

6. Talk to yourself as you would a sibling or a friend.

7. See the gifts in your challenges.

8. Realize that feeling the full range of emotions is not something you have to "fix."

9. See yourself as a work in progress.

10. Accept yourself in action (and model it for others).

11. Create stillness to feel more at ease with yourself.

12. Use your judgments as a mirror to grow into greater self-acceptance.

13. Reframe guilt- and shame-driven thoughts to be more self-compassionate.

14. Realize your mistakes only define you if you let them.

15. Remove the phrase "should have" from your vocabulary.

16. Ask yourself how you can respond more wisely than you have in the past.

17. When you deal with rejection, recognize in what ways you're rejecting yourself.

18. Challenge your assumption that other people are judging you.

19. See it as a positive sign if some people don't like you.

20. Keep a self-appreciation journal.

21. Flip your focus from what you *aren't* to what you *are*.

22. Stop the fearful mental stories that lead into self-destructive mental territory.

23. Get excited by what you can do instead of discouraged by what you think you can't.

24. Focus on what you can enjoy right now.

25. Use the mantra "I am loved" if you feel the urge to cling to other people.

26. Challenge your fears around love so you don't end up settling for an unhealthy relationship.

27. Identify your core values and priorities to better know, understand, and love yourself.

28. Treat yourself as you want a partner to treat you.

29. See yourself beyond your roles.

30. Take a tiny step to move beyond your mask.

31. Challenge yourself to be vulnerable.

32. Ask yourself, "What is my shadow side trying to tell me?"

33. Nurture yourself from the inside out.

34. Be gentle with yourself if you experience resistance.

35. Make a list of your top needs.

36. Practice saying no when a request would impact your ability to take care of yourself.

37. Ask yourself, "What would make me proud of myself if I weren't trying to impress other people?"

38. Experiment with what gives you energy.

39. Create a vision and take tiny steps toward fulfilling it each day.

40. Look back at where you were ten years ago, five years ago, and one year ago to celebrate how far you've come.

THE QUOTES

*You, yourself, as much as anybody in the entire universe,
deserve your love and affection.*

—BUDDHA

Pain is inevitable. Suffering is optional.

—UNKNOWN

*When there is no enemy within, the enemies outside
cannot hurt you.*

—AFRICAN PROVERB

Because of your smile, you make life more beautiful.

—THICH NHAT HANH

No matter where you go, there you are.

—Confucius

The most important thing in this world is to learn to give out love, and let it come in.

—Morrie Schwartz

It isn't what happens to us that causes us to suffer; it's what we say to ourselves about what happens.

—Pema Chödrön

It is better to be whole than to be good.

—John Middleton Murray

Good enough is the new perfect.

—Becky Beaupre Gillespie and
Hollee Schwartz Temple

To be beautiful means to be yourself. You don't need to be accepted by others. You need to accept yourself.

—THICH NHAT HANH

The moment you accept yourself you become beautiful.

—OSHO

If we learn to open our hearts, anyone, including the people who drive us crazy, can be our teacher.

—PEMA CHÖDRÖN

Be gentle first with yourself if you wish to be gentle with others.

—LAMA YESHE

Things and conditions can give you pleasure but they cannot give you joy—joy arises from within.

—ECKHART TOLLE

Tension is who you think you should be. Relaxation is who you are.

—Proverb

When you lose, don't lose the lesson.

—Unknown

Your task is not to seek love, but merely to seek and find all the barriers within yourself that you have built against it.

—Rumi

What I am is good enough if I would only be it openly.

—Carl Rogers

What other people think of me is none of my business.

—Wayne Dyer

Criticism is something you can easily avoid by saying nothing,
doing nothing, being nothing

—ARISTOTLE

It takes courage to grow up and become who you really are.

—E. E. CUMMINGS

The greater part of human pain is unnecessary. It is self-created
as long as the unobserved mind runs your life.

—ECKHART TOLLE

Why compare yourself with others? No one in the entire world
can do a better job of being you than you.

—UNKNOWN

If you worry about what might be, and wonder what might
have been, you will ignore what is.

—UNKNOWN

As long as you make an identity for yourself out of pain, you cannot be free of it.

—ECKHART TOLLE

We love because it is the only true adventure.

—NIKKI GIOVANNI

If you make friends with yourself, you will never be alone.

—MAXWELL MALTZ

You, yourself, as much as anybody in the entire universe, deserve your love and affection.

—BUDDHA

Don't think you're on the right road just because it's a well-beaten path.

—UNKNOWN

Our lives only improve when we are willing to take chances and the first and most difficult risk we can take is to be honest with ourselves.

—WALTER ANDERSON

What makes you vulnerable makes you beautiful.

—BRENÉ BROWN

Man stands in his own shadow and wonders why it's dark.

—ZEN PROVERB

Be gentle with yourself. You are a child of the universe, no less than the trees and the stars. In the noisy confusion of life, keep peace in your soul.

—MAX EHRMANN

Have respect for yourself, and patience and compassion. With these, you can handle anything.

—JACK KORNFIELD

The way you treat yourself sets the standard for others.
—Dr. Sonya Friedman

You don't have to worry about burning bridges if you're building your own.
—Kerry E. Wagner

Your outlook on life is a direct reflection on how much you like yourself.
—lululemon

And in the end, it's not the years in your life that count. It's the life in your years.
—Abraham Lincoln

The grass is always greener where you water it.

—UNKNOWN

Always concentrate on how far you've come, rather than how far you have left to go.

—UNKNOWN

THE STORIES

THE CONTRIBUTORS

Alesha Chilton

Alesha Chilton is an MBA graduate who enjoys writing to help others. Her recent book about relationships titled *The System for Women: Find and Keep the Man of Your Dreams Online!* is available on Amazon. Visit Alesha atchicandcraftydiva.com.

Alexandra Heather Foss

Alexandra Heather Foss is a freelance writer whose writing has been featured on Tiny Buddha and in *The New York Times*. What time is not spent creating word art is spent with divine nature—of herself, others, the cosmos, and this special planet we call home.

Alison Hummel

Alison Hummel is the founder of thedreamadventure.com and lives in Philadelphia with her husband Jon, their son Cash, and their cat, Kittie. She is dedicated to pursuing her own dreams and encouraging others to pursue theirs.

Amyra Mah

Amyra Mah is a spiritual coach, intuitive counselor, writer, blogger, and creator of extraordinary programs for addictions and other lifestyle imbalances. She is passionate about helping people find unusual sources of power, spiritual meaning, and a profound sense of comfort within, so that they rise to their magnificence. Visit her at theamyrarecords.com.

An Bourmanne

An Bourmanne loves mentoring people-pleasing perfectionists to confidently and unapologetically do their thing in the world and create a sizzling life that makes their heart sing and soar. She rediscovered her long-lost love for teaching and writing, which she does weekly at ownyourlifecoaching.com.

Angela Gunn

Angela Gunn is an award-winning writer based in Savannah, Georgia, who specializes in screenwriting and online and print media. She completed her second novel for NaNoWriMo 2012 and is currently working on a children's book, which will be published in 2013. Her writing and contact information can be found at angegunn.com.

Cat Li Stevenson

Cat Li Stevenson is a devotee to wellness, mindfulness, and happiness, and a recent corporate escapee who is living and practicing Zen, for the next year or so, on various meditation cushions in the world. At the intersection of her dynamic roles, Cat blogs at thinksimplenow.com. Add her as a friend on Facebook (facebook.com/catherine.l.stevenson) or follow her on Twitter @Cat_Stevenson.

Charlie Tranchemontagne

Charlie Tranchemontagne is a work (life) in progress. He's looking to find his own voice through writing and sharing, continuing to find himself on the road of self-discovery, and connecting with fellow travelers.

Elizabeth Garbee

Elizabeth Garbee is a college student who loves her brother, her cats, and playing the violin. She's a regular reader of Tiny Buddha.

Emma Brooke

Emma Brooke is a hypnotherapist, yoga lover, and counselor living life without regrets. She wants to change the world but still gets a bit scared about how to do it. She is super proud of being independent but still loves a cuddle from someone who believes in her. Follow her on Twitter @emmabr00ke and visit her at emmabrooke.co.uk.

Erin Lanahan

Erin Lanahan is an internationally certified holistic health coach, personal trainer, yoga instructor, motivational writer and speaker, and life empowerment mentor. Her mission is to inspire as many people as possible to return to their natural state of peace, abundance, health, inspiration, and love. Visit her blog at erinlanahanmethod.com and her YouTube page at youtube.com/user/ErinLanahanMethod.

Hannah Braime

Hannah Braime runs the blog Becoming Who You Are (becomingwhoyouare.net), a guide to authentic living. She is passionate about helping people create the lives they want from the inside out. She is the author of two books, *The Ultimate Guide to Journaling* and *The Ultimate Guide to Sentence Completion.* Connect with her on Facebook at facebook.com/becomingwhoyouare and on Twitter @becomewhour.

Jaclyn Witt

Jaclyn Witt is a twenty-something born with a rare form of muscular dystrophy. She lives in Southern California and works for a travel company. Her blog, imaspiring.wordpress.com, details what it's like being a single female living with a disability. She hopes her story will inspire others.

Jarl Forsman

In her journey of self-awareness, Jarl Forsman has found a way of thinking to help peacefully navigate the sometimes tumultuous seas of life. She cofounded the website gratitudetwentyfourseven.com to provide free daily insights and other tools to help others expand their self-awareness, overcome limiting beliefs, and rediscover the happiness within.

Jeanine Nicole

Jeanine Nicole is a writer, goal coach, personal growth teacher, and yoga instructor who lives in New York City. She blogs at zestforthequest. com. You can reach her at jeaninenicole@zestforthequest.com or on Twitter @ZestfortheQuest. Learn more at beginwithin18.com.

Jenni Hanley

Jenni Hanley is a freelance writer and editor. In addition to blogging about locally grown food at eatthisdallas.net, she is a contributor for *Renfrew Connections,* a newsletter providing hope, help, and healing to those struggling with eating disorders.

Jennifer Chrisman

Jennifer Chrisman is a licensed clinical psychologist practicing in Los Angeles. She specializes in using mindfulness-based approaches to help her clients find more meaning in their life. Visit her website at drjenniferchrisman.com, or follow her on Facebook at facebook.com/drjennchrisman or on Twitter @drjennchrisman.

Jennifer Gargotto

Jennifer Gargotto is an online marketing and SEO professional living in Denver, Colorado. You can follow her adventures online at msmorphosis.com, where she writes about fearless thinking for modern women, and bloggingfearlessly.com, where she teaches people how to grow personally and professionally online.

Joanna Z. Weston

Joanna Z. Weston is passionate about helping people recovering from depression to build a life they can love. She would love to guide you through the awkward space between depression and wellness. You can find her bicycling through the streets of Boston, snuggling her cat, reading voraciously, and blogging at 3speedlife.com.

Julia Manuel

Julia Manuel is a writer and strategic communications specialist in Northern Virginia. An assistant with a Baptiste-affiliated yoga studio, she hopes to empower students to achieve unity between mind and body while giving back to the community that has helped her live authentically. She contributes to her yoga studio's blog, focusing on wellness and inquiry.

Julie Hoyle

Julie Hoyle is a spiritual teacher, natural intuitive, and transpersonal hypnotherapist. Her profound spiritual awakening is detailed in her e-book, *An Awakened Life: A Journey of Transformation.* She offers online courses, soul purpose readings, and energy retrieval at truealignment.org.

Katy Cowan

Katy Cowan is an author, journalist, and marketing professional based in the United Kingdom. She runs a marketing consultancy in Manchester called Boomerang (weareboomerang.com) and during her spare time she loves to help other creatives via her online industry magazine *Creative Boom* (creativeboom.co.uk).

Kayla Albert

Kayla Albert is a social media specialist by day and a personal growth blogger by night. You can follow her on Twitter @KaylaAlbert33 or check out more of her writing at kaylaalbert.com.

Kaylee Rupp

Kaylee Rupp's quest is helping others create purposeful, authentic, passionate lives—without the stress. For peaceful strategies (and a bit of whimsy), visit her at zencaffeine.com.

Lisa Stefany

Lisa Stefany is a proud graduate of Penn State University. She majored in English and minors in wearing patterns that clash and colors that don't quite match. She galvanizes her mind with yoga, wine, and grasping at the absurd intricacies of quantum mechanics, inflating universe(s), bizarre bacteria, and epigenetics.

Lucy H. Pearce

Lucy H. Pearce is the author of several books, including *Moon Time: A Guide to Celebrating Your Menstrual Cycle* and founder of *The Happy Womb* (thehappywomb.com) for empowering women's resources. She blogs on creativity, mindfulness, and motherhood at dreamingaloud.net. Connect with Lucy on Facebook at facebook.com/

DreamingAloudNt and facebook.com/thehappywomb and on Twitter @DreamingAloudNt.

Madison Sonnier

Madison Sonnier is an aspiring writer and lover of animals, music, nature, and creativity. She loves to read, write, and spend time with her dogs. You can follow her on Twitter @MyLyricQuotes or her blog at journeyofasoulsearcher.blogspot.com.

Maelina Frattaroli

Maelina Frattaroli was born knowing she wanted to pursue writing. She believes most of life's complexities can be cured through the written word, listening to Neil Diamond, and garlic-infused dishes. In her spare time she writes poetry, hikes mountains, and wines and dines with good company. A garlic tattoo on her inner ankle is her pride and joy.

Margie Beiswanger

Margie teaches service-oriented entrepreneurs how to translate their unique expertise into signature programs and products so they can reach more of their ideal clients, leverage their time, expand their business, and earn a good living. She's passionate about showing people how their brilliance can shine even brighter! Visit her at transformyourbrilliance.com.

Marie

Marie is an avid reader and occasional contributor to thesatiricalstylist.com.

Mary Dunlop

Mary Dunlop is a passionate student of life with a keen desire to learn, share, and grow. She believes everyone has a special gift. Hers is writing, and currently she is publishing her first novella, *The Beauty of Twin Flame Love.*

Michelle Ghilotti Mandel

Michelle Ghilotti Mandel helps women make happiness their business, locally and abroad. She is a branding expert, motivational speaker, writer, consultant and coach. She is currently working on her latest book, *How to Be a Walking Momtra.* Visit her at michelleghilotti.com.

Michael Davidson

Michael Davidson writes about how to live a healthy and happy life at *www.feelhappiness.com.* Follow him on Twitter @feelhappinessMD.

Patrycja Domurad

Patrycja Domurad is a writer living in Toronto, Canada. She attributes her strengths to: losing her eye in a car accident at fourteen, and living with a facial difference since; triumphing over personal demons; and finding love. She lives her dream by inspiring people to challenge their beliefs about their lives and seek greatness. Follow her at inspiredgreatness.tumblr.com.

Sacha Crouch

Author of *De-stress Your Success: Get More of What You Want with Less Time, Stress and Effort,* Sacha Crouch is a business executive, life coach, and an expert in work-life balance.

Sam Russell

Sam Russell is a writer living in a corner of the United Kingdom. A cynic by nature, Sam's proving that cynics can be happy and positive, too. Visit his blog at cackhanded.wordpress.com.

Sarah Louise Byrne

Sarah Louise Byrne is a women's empowerment writer who blogs at sarah-queen.com. She is also the content editor for Careershifters.org. You can follow Sarah on Twitter @QueenSarah.

Sheila Prakash

Sheila Prakash passionately believes in everyone's ability to open their hearts and heal their hurts in order to discover and share their light. As a psychospiritual therapist and transpersonal breathwork facilitator she guides people on their journey of self-discovery. Learn more at lookingwithintherapy.com.

Stephen Light

Stephen Light loves people and sees them for their potential, not the behaviors they display. His purpose is to connect, share, serve, and grow. He sees his life as a journey and loves that he can make a difference in people's lives. Visit him at peopleactiv.com, on Twitter @bringinglight1, or on Facebook (search Stephen Light—Bringing the Light).

Wendy Miyake

Wendy Miyake is an author, teacher, and lover of life's journey. Her new life's motto is: if everything were perfect, you wouldn't remember anything. Follow her new blog momochanconquerstheworld.com and look for her forthcoming children's picture book on loss called *The Sky Blanket*.

ABOUT THE AUTHOR

LORI DESCHENE HAS DEDICATED THE LAST four years of her life building a supportive online community for those seeking and looking to share wisdom. Since she launched tinybuddha.com in 2009, she's helped more than 650 writers share their stories with over 17 million readers.

In addition to writing her first print book, *Tiny Buddha: Simple Wisdom for Life's Hard Questions*, Lori has self-published the Tiny Wisdom eBook series, and recently launched her first eCourse, Recreate Your Life Story: Change the Script and Be the Hero (recreateyourlifestory.com). Formerly a writer for nationally distributed 'tween publications, she has also written articles for *Tricycle: The Buddhist Review*, *Shambhala Sun*, and *Chicken Soup for the Soul*.

A native of Massachusetts, Lori now splits her time between the Boston area and the San Francisco Bay Area with her fiancé Ehren.

TO OUR READERS